All About Finches

and Related Seed-Eating Birds

Ian Harman and Dr. Matthew M. Vriends

Pictorial Credits:

Black and white:
Charles R. Fisher: 18.
Otto Hansen: 4.
Harry V. Lacey: 1, 7, 16, 26, 28, 32, 79, 99, 101, 102, 123, 130, 144, 151, 153, 158, 165, 171, 187, 190, 191, 192, 193, 194, 201, 216, 217.
Louise van der Meid: 13, 15, 20, 21, 24, 25, 27, 30, 51, 58, 62, 160, 183, 185, 206, 207, 208, 209, 215.
Horst Mueller: 119, 121, 199, 211, 212.
Prevue Metal Products, Inc., Chicago, Ill.: 12, 14.

Color:
Harry V. Lacey: 33, 44.
Horst Mueller: 34, 35, 41, 45 (top), 52, 53, 56, 57, 60, 61, 65 (below), 68, 72 (below), 76, 77, 80 (below), 81, 84, 85 (below), 96.
Louise van der Meid: 40, 45 (below), 65 (top), 69, 72 (top), 73, 80 (top), 85 (top), 88, 89, 92, 93.

Drawings by R. A. Vowles

Cover Photo by Horst Mueller

Based on *Finches* by Ian Harman.

© Copyright 1978 by T.F.H. Publications, Inc. Ltd.

ISBN 0-87666-965-8

Distributed in the U.S. by T.F.H. Publications, Inc., 211 West Sylvania Avenue, P.O. Box 427, Neptune, N.J. 07753; in England by T.F.H. (Gt. Britain) Ltd., 13 Nutley Lane, Reigate, Surrey; in Canada to the book store and library trade by Clarke, Irwin & Company, Clarwin House, 791 St. Clair Avenue West, Toronto 10, Ontario; in Canada to the pet trade by Rolf C. Hagen Ltd., 3225 Sartelon Street, Montreal 382, Quebec; in Southeast Asia by Y.W. Ong, 9 Lorong 36 Geylang, Singapore 14; in Australia and the South Pacific by Pet Imports Pty. Ltd., P.O. Box 149, Brookvale 2100, N.S.W., Australia; in South Africa by Valiant Publishers (Pty.) Ltd., P.O. Box 78236, Sandton City, 2146, South Africa; Published by T.F.H. Publications, Inc., Ltd., The British Crown Colony of Hong Kong.

Contents

Bishop (*E. capensis*); Red-billed Weaver (*Quelea quelea*); Rufous-necked Weaver (*Ploceus cucullatus*); Cape Weaver (*Ploceus capensis*); Half-masked Weaver (*Ploceus velatus*); Little Masked Weaver (*P. luteola*); Thick-billed Weaver (*Amblyospiza albifrons*); Baya Weaver (*Ploceus philippinus*); Pintail Whydah (*Vidua macroura*); Long-tailed Combassou (*V. hypocherina*); Shaft-tailed Whydah (*V. regia*); Red-collared Whydah (*Euplectes ardens*); Giant Whydah (*E. progne*); White-winged Whydah (*E. albonotatus*); Yellow-backed Whydah (*E. macrourus*); Red-shouldered Whydah (*E. axillaris*); Paradise Whydah (*Steganura paradisea*); Jackson's Whydah (*Euplectes jacksoni*); Senegal Combassou (*Hypochera chalybeata*); Tree Sparrow (*Passer montanus*); Golden Sparrow (*P. luteus*).

Cordon Bleu (*Uraeginthus bengalus*); Blue-breasted Waxbill (*U. angolensis*); Violet-eared Waxbill (*U. granatina*); Red-eared Waxbill (*Estrilda troglodytes*); St. Helena Waxbill (*E. astrild*); Black-cheeked Waxbill (*E. erythronotus*); Lavender Finch (*Lagonosticta caerulescens*); Red-browed Waxbill (*Aegintha temporalis*); Gold-breasted Waxbill (*Amandava subflava*); Orange-cheeked Waxbill (*Estrilda melpoda*); Avadavat or Tiger Finch (*Amandava amandava*); Green Avadavat (*A. formosa*); Fire-finch (*Lagonosticta senegala*); Jameson's Fire-finch (*L. jamesoni*); Peter's Twinspot (*Hypargos niveoguttatus*); Melba Finch (*Pytilia melba*); Aurora Finch (*P. phoenicoptera*); Dufresne's Waxbill (*Estrilda melanotis*); Quail Finch (*Ortygospiza atricollis*); Scaly-crowned Finch (*Sporopipes squamifrons*).

Gouldian Finch (*Chloebia gouldiae*); Long-tailed Grass-finch (*Poephila acuticauda*); Parson Finch (*P. cincta*); Masked Finch (*P. personata*); Zebra Finch (*P. guttata*); Star Finch (*P. ruficauda*); Diamond Sparrow (*Zonaeginthus guttatus*); Fire-tailed Finch (*Z. bellus*); Painted Finch (*Z. picta*); Bicheno Finch (*Stizoptera bichenovii*); Plumhead Finch (*Aidemosyne modesta*); Crimson Finch (*Poephila phaeton*); Pin-tailed Parrot Finch (*Erythrura prasina*); Red-headed Parrot Finch (*E. psittacea*); Blue-faced Parrot Finch (*E. trichroa*); Royal Parrot Finch (*E. regia*); Java Sparrow (*Padda oryzivora*); Black-headed Mannikin (*Lonchura atricapilla*); Spicebird or Nutmeg Finch (*L. punctulata*); Bengalese or Society Finch (*L. striata*); African Silverbill (*L. cantans*); Cut-throat Finch (*Amadina fasciata*); Magpie Mannikin (*Lonchura fringilloides*); Bronze Mannikin (*L. cucullata*); Yellow-rumped Finch (*L. flavipyrmna*); Chestnut-breasted Finch (*L. castaneothorax*); Pictorella Finch (*L. pectoralis*).

I General Management

Aviaries

Birds can be kept in cages or aviaries, both indoors and out. For most kinds of finches, outdoor aviaries are by far the most satisfactory, and every fancier ought to try and find room in his garden for at least one small aviary. Finches are seldom kept permanently in cages these days. They live and appear quite happy in cages of generous size, but such birds are far more interesting in an aviary, and the pleasure that their owner will derive from watching a happy company of these gay feathered creatures disporting themselves therein, and going about their business of rearing families, has to be experienced to be fully appreciated.

Outdoor aviaries are roughly divided into two types: those which are intended to house a mixed collection, and those divided into compartments, or pens, for the separation of breeding pairs. While a great many birds will breed satisfactorily in the community aviary, others prove vicious, quarrelsome or interfering in mixed company. These are best housed with birds which are not near natural relations, or, where possible, in pairs apart from other birds. Such species are indicated under their respective headings in the text.

However, it may be mentioned here that birds of different sizes should not, as a rule, be kept together, though size is much less important than natural disposition. Some big birds are quite inoffensive, whereas some small species are very aggressive. Birds closely related to each other and those of similar coloring do not often agree. For example, Virginian Cardinals and Scarlet Tanagers never get on well and may fight to the death. Red-crested and Pope Cardinals are also impossible companions. Budgerigars should never be allowed to associate with other birds.

Individuals among birds differ considerably in temperament, so that it is impossible to lay down hard-and-fast rules for the association of different species of birds. However, any of the following small foreign finches ought to be safe together, provided they are not overcrowded:

5

Fire Finches, Orange-cheeked, Gold-breasted and St. Helena Waxbills, Cordon Bleus, Green and Gray Singing Finches, Zebra Finches, all the Australian finches except the Crimson Finch, Avadavats, Bengalese, Silverbills, Cuban or Olive Finches, but not both. Mannikins of most species, Lavender Finches, Melba Finches, Saffron Finches, Rainbow, Versicolor and Nonpareil Buntings. Small insectivorous birds such as sugar birds, Pekin Robins, small tanagers and the like are quite safe companions in an aviary of small foreign finches. The smaller doves, such as Diamond and Masked varieties, and various kinds of quail also go well with this finch collection, and add variety. Some fanciers keep Golden or Lady Amherst Pheasants with the smallest foreign finches, and find the big birds do not harm their small companions.

Another collection could consist of weavers and whydahs, cardinals, Java Sparrows, Cut-throats, and the larger British finches. The main requirements of all outdoor aviaries in temperate climates are that they should have an entirely closed-in shelter provided with windows to admit light, and a door through which the attendant can enter. The birds gain access to the attached flight through a small door, or pigeon-holes, which can be closed with a wooden slide when necessary. Most birds like to retire to the closed part of the aviary for part of the day, especially in dull, wet weather, as well as using it for sleeping.

It is unwise to allow birds to sleep in the open flight, as heavy rains, cats, owls and other enemies may scare them and result in deaths among your stock. If birds are driven into their sleeping quarters a few times, they will soon become accustomed to retiring there at dusk of their own accord.

Apart from the closed portion, the aviary really consists only of a flight, which should be mostly half-inch wire netting. The ideal aviary has part of the open flight covered over the top, but beyond that is all-open wire-netted flight. The top of the aviary should preferably not be entirely covered unless the aviary is quite small. Finches love to sit out in the sunshine, and this greatly invigorates them. This is particularly true of the Australian species.

Plants should only be grown in large open flights, and not in small portable-type aviaries. In the latter they so quickly become fouled with the birds' droppings that they are only an eyesore.

In many cases, the modern aviary consists of two adjoining parts, namely a wired-in or glassed-in flight and a roofed-over permanent shelter or house attached to it.

Many fanciers prefer to construct their own aviaries, but in Europe numerous specialist firms offer sectional aviaries which are sent out all ready for erection.

The size of the aviary will have to be left to the direction of the individual fancier, but it may be mentioned that good breeding successes have been achieved in quite small aviaries. A large aviary that is overcrowded will probably give poorer breeding results

Finches and the like may usually be kept together in the same aviary, provided it affords them plenty of room for flying, mating, and breeding activities. After years of costly experience, we have learned that it pays to respect the individual characteristics and habits of each species by keeping it in a compartment by itself. Such separation has the added advantage of giving the fancier a good opportunity to study the various feeding, breeding, and other requirements of each avian variety.

than a small one with a few good pairs of birds. As far as finches are concerned, the only advantage of a very large aviary is that the birds may find more natural live food on which to rear their young and more natural nesting sites if growing shrubs are planted in the open flight. Some finches, though seed eaters when adult, feed their young entirely on insect fare, and breeding results will not be achieved unless they are able to obtain this or unless it is provided. But others can rear their young on a simple diet of seed, dry or soaked, with some bread-and-milk or soft-bill mixture.

Aviaries can be of any shape but in a small garden we advise the construction of a long, narrow aviary. This gives the birds room for a good flight and is more attractive than a square structure. Be sure that the aviary gets some sunshine and that it is protected from cold winds.

When setting up an aviary make it rat-proof. In small aviaries this can be done by covering the whole of the site where it is to stand with one-half inch wire netting. Use enough to permit it to extend a foot or so beyond the aviary all around the sides. This extra length should then be brought up to the lower part of the boarding and secured there with staples. This will stop rats from burrowing up underneath or chewing their way through the bottom part should the woodwork become rotted. This netting should be treated with tar to prevent its deterioration through rust.

Another method of making an aviary rat-proof, which does not require so much wire netting, is to put a trench of it all around the structure. To do this dig a trench about a foot deep and eighteen inches wide all around the aviary. Tack wire netting about a foot above ground level to the sides of the aviary, carry this down to the bottom of the trench and bend it outward along the floor of the trench. Then fill up the trench with earth, throwing in as many broken bricks, stones, and similar materials as you can lay hands on. This also helps to drain the aviary site.

Mice are less easy to exclude from aviaries. These creatures seldom actually harm the birds, but they foul and eat their food, disturb them at night, and damage nests. Mice can be kept out by the use of three-eighths inch wire netting, but it is seldom obtainable nowadays. Young mice can easily get through the ordinary one-half inch mesh.

Break-back mouse traps can be set, and these should be placed under an upturned box, with only a small hole through which the mice can enter. Where aviaries are placed on a raised platform or terrace adjoining a path, mice can be prevented from gaining an entry by fixing a continuous ridge of wood or metal along the sides. This should be about six inches wide, slanting outward and downward, and placed below the part where the wire netting begins.

The type of material for aviary floors is largely a matter of personal choice. The sleeping quarters of sectional aviaries usually have wooden floors. For the flight, one can have bare earth, sand, wood, concrete or tiles. Bare earth becomes soiled in time, and has to be dug over, or the top layer replaced. Also, an earth floor becomes very messy in wet weather, especially where a flight is

Outdoor aviaries are by far the
most satisfactory. An aviary is a
reasonably large enclosure
usually placed outdoors, with
one or more sides (walls) made
of wire, glass or wood or other
more or less 'open' or
transparent material. Its purpose
is to house a number of birds
satisfactorily the year round.

covered only with wire netting. Of course, grass can be grown in aviaries with very large flights. A sand-covered floor is quite satisfactory in very small aviaries which have the whole of the roof boarded over against the weather. But by far the best type of floor covering is concrete or tiles. This can be covered with a layer of sand, which can be swept off periodically and replaced with fresh. An earth floor to the sleeping quarters higher than the ground around the aviary is generally quite satisfactory.

The newly erected aviary should be coated on the outside with creosote. It is quite safe to use creosote on the inside of aviaries, but it tends to make the sleeping quarters rather dark. For the inside of aviaries, the best paint to use is washable distemper, or flat paint such as is used for undercoating. Make sure all paint and creosote is perfectly dry before putting any birds in the aviary.

Aviary furnishings should be of a simple, practical nature. Perches for the sleeping quarters should consist of wooden curtain rods for small birds and dowels for larger ones.

These should be placed high up near the roof. For the flight, natural, twiggy branches make the best perches. Prunings from fruit trees are ideal to use. Fix the perches firmly but not too permanently, as they will probably have to be removed after a year or so of use. Perches in the open flight are washed fairly clean by rain; those under cover will have to be scrubbed regularly. Never allow perches to become fouled for long, or your birds will contact ailments, as they are constantly wiping their beaks on the perches.

The sizes of outdoor aviaries vary enormously, and they may be anything from six to sixty feet or more in length. The most popular size for small town gardens is about ten or twelve feet in length, six feet wide, and about seven feet high. The minimum amount of space allotted to a bird the size of a canary should be one square foot.

Cages

Perhaps the best type of cage in which to house finches is the ordinary canary double breeding cage, about thirty-six inches by fourteen inches by ten inches wide, and no birds ought to be kept permanently in cages smaller than this. Several small finches could be associated in such a cage. The box-type cage with the front of wire is the best to adopt. The all-wire ornamental cage is

The standard canary cage is suitable for a pair of small finches or two unrelated but congenial species.

All-wire ornamental cages are popular with those fanciers who keep just one or two birds as living room pets, but they are unpopular with serious birdlovers.

popular with those who keep just one or two birds as drawing room pets, but they are unpopular with the serious fancier. For one thing, birds lodged in such cages are exposed to all drafts and are much more easily frightened than when kept in a box cage.

All-wire cages are easy to clean, but if this task is to be really simple, there should be no fancy work attached to the cage at all, as one soon learns in practice that the more decoration and ornamentation, the more difficult it is really to get down to the task of a thorough cleaning.

Such cages, too, are seldom large enough to make a satisfactory permanent home for birds.

Perches are a very important point in the equipment of cages. Many fanciers favor using natural branches, so that the birds are not always grasping a hard piece of wood of the same size. Perches are more often too small than too large, and these should be of such a size that the bird can grasp them easily, without having to grip them so tightly that the back and front claws meet.

All-wire cages afford little protection to the bird from drafts which can be, and often are, fatal. Pay great attention to the situation of the cage in the room.

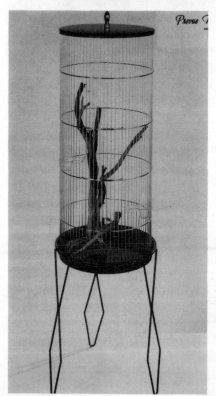

In this cage the birds are exposed on all sides and there is really no place in which they can find seclusion. A timid bird, when approached, will most likely panic. To avoid this place an open cage close to a wall to provide it with a solid back, although you will lose much of the apparent virtue of an all-wire cage.

Two perches are usually enough in an ordinary box cage, set one at each end. Do not, however, place the perches so close to the ends of the cage that the bird rubs its tail against the woodwork at every turn.

Bird-rooms

The main advantage of having a bird-room is that one can maintain in a temperate or cold climate many species of birds which are not sufficiently hardy in constitution to winter in outdoor aviaries. For the canary fancier, of course, a bird-room is an essential, since canaries generally are not bred in aviaries.

Birds of many different types and sizes can be kept in cages in the same room, whereas a number of aviaries would be needed to house them out-of-doors. For the finch fancier, a bird-room is useful for housing the more delicate species through the winter, though it is not necessary in the southern states, or in warmer climates, as South Africa and Australia.

A bird-room, too, is a pleasant place for the fancier to while away his leisure hours during the winter evenings when he would have little opportunity of watching birds in outdoor aviaries. Many keen fanciers have a small bird-room as well as outdoor aviaries.

Oriental cages for a pair of finches; although very attractive in appearance they are regarded by most fanciers as inadequate.

A beautiful garden birdroom for finches, such as Lady Goulds and other Australian finches.

Back view of batteries of all-metal breeding cages with daylight lighting for winter use. All feeding, cleaning, etc., is done from behind. Each cage has an inclined tray beneath its wire bottom;this permits all droppings, seed husks, and other refuse which has fallen through the wire to be easily swept to the end.

A suggestion for a simple indoor enclosure. Fresh air in inside bird-rooms is usually provided by either windows or special ventilators.

Bird-rooms may be indoor or outdoor. The former is usually a spare attic or store room, fitted up with staging to hold cages round the best lighted walls. Such a room must be free from drafts and dampness, and should preferably not have a northerly or northeasterly aspect. A room facing south often becomes too hot in summer. Where a bird-room has a very sunny aspect, an outside blind should be fitted, made to work on rollers, so that it can be let down in hot weather. An inside blind is of little use, and though it shields the inmates from the direct rays of the sun it does not protect the room from becoming hot and stifling.

Outdoor bird-rooms are by far the most popular. These are well-made sheds, lined and fitted with large windows, made to open, or removable. All windows, by the way, in bird-rooms and aviaries, should be protected with wire netting. Sometimes a part of the bird-room is wired off with netting, so as to form an aviary or flight. This is very useful as an exercise room for young birds, which develop better under such conditions than in cages.

Electricity is a boon in the bird-room, not only for providing good lighting during the dark winter evenings, but for heating purposes. The ideal method of heating is by heaters controlled by thermostats. When there is no current available, fumeless heaters can be used. Birds are better able to adapt themselves to different climates than many other creatures, and most of the commonly imported kinds from the tropics will winter with little or no artificial heating. Nevertheless, it is as well to provide some heat during the very cold spells of weather.

Care of Birds

Birds are easy creatures to manage, and the basic requirements are that they should be kept under clean conditions and fed regularly with suitable food. The daily cleaning out of the sand-tray in the case of birds kept in cages is a task which must not be overlooked. Most birds spend a good deal of time on the floor of their cages, and if they begin to pick up scraps of food befouled with droppings, disease will be likely to break out among them sooner or later.

Birds should be handled as little as possible, but if unavoidable this should be carefully done. Experienced fanciers catch birds

A popular carrying cage for one or two small birds. Close wire spacing prevents escape of even the smallest finch. For birds which panic easily, the cage should be covered on all sides to prevent injury.

with the hand, but if you are not used to handling birds, try the following method. Cover the cage with a cloth or sack and allow time for the inmates to settle down. Then raise a corner of the covering, note the position the bird you want has taken up, and quietly insert the hand, grasp it around the back, over the wings, gently but firmly. When caught in this way there is no risk of any damage being done, as may be the case when no cover is used. Birds in aviaries can be caught in suitable nets. The ring of the nets should be covered with rubber gas tubing.

When buying birds, care must be taken to select only the active, bright-eyed specimens, without traces of bowel looseness. This is often no easy task, especially with nervous species and in cases where they are too overcrowded to permit of free movement. When a dealer catches a bird for you, see that the undertail parts are clean and that the breast is plump and well filled but not overly fat. Always examine the legs and feet in case there are toes missing or lumps or sores present.

In cases where the sexes are similar in color and size, it is a difficult task to get a true pair. Experienced dealers and breeders get to know the cocks from the hens without really knowing any particular points of difference. Often a good dealer can pick out a pair, and if you know your man leave the selection to him.

With certain birds, especially immature birds, pairs can only be selected with some amount of luck. The best plan is to select a couple of birds which are as dissimilar as possible, particularly in head size, and have them put together in a cage for a few minutes.

Equipment for aviaries consists, for example, of perches, waterers, baths, feeders, nest-boxes, etc. There is much choice and variation. Ask your pet shop for professional advice.

If they seem friendly, the chances are they will prove to be a true pair. Sometimes birds which are alike have different call notes.

Birds are often bought from advertisements. They travel well by rail or air transport. They are generally sent in shallow wooden boxes, with a few holes for air, and a perch or two fixed near the floor. Seed is generally scattered on the floor, but birds are quite

Perches should fit the feet of the finches. Hardwood per-ches are easily installed and easily scraped clean with a perch cleaner. When perch covers are used one does not have to worry about trimming the nails of the birds.

often disinclined to eat during short journeys. More elaborate traveling cages, with water and wire fronts to admit light, are required for journeys longer than a day.

Newly received birds should be immediately turned into a cage, even if received late at night, when a good light should be left on near the cage till morning. Water is the first thing they should be given, and then some seed and perhaps a few meal worms. Birds

Feeders in many variations are available at your local pet store. Some of the feeders and dishes are especially attractive and useful. Select as many as will be necessary to supply the different foods one will be offering.

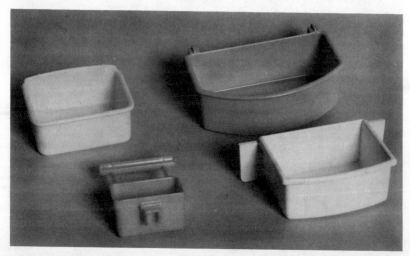

newly purchased should not be put into an aviary straight away, unless you know they have come from a similar habitation and are perfectly healthy and fit. Most fanciers have a quarantine cage into which all newly bought birds are put for a few days. This is a wise safeguard against introducing infectious diseases among your stock.

With some tropical birds there is always some risk if newly imported specimens are purchased, due to the need for carefully acclimatizing them. Many species do not require any greater heat than an ordinary livingroom temperature, even when first imported, and if placed in an outdoor aviary about the end of May—according to local climatic conditions—will be able to remain there permanently without heat.

But a few kinds are never able to withstand conditions out-of-doors, except during the spring, summer and autumn. These will have to be wintered in a bird-room, with heating available.

Finch food consists of four parts of small Australian millet, two parts of plain canary or white seed, one part white proso millet, and one half part oat groats. Some mixtures also include niger; this seed is best offered in a separate dish.

This is not the right way! These imported Rice Birds (and a Cut-throat finch on the right) are naturally easily alarmed, so it is a sound idea to put them in comparatively small cages at first. This allows the owner to inspect the birds very carefully for possible signs of ill health.

Regarding this question of hardiness, readers must make allowances according to where they live. A bird stated in this book to be hardy means that it may safely be wintered in a climate not more severe than the south of England. Many birds which fanciers in Britain find to be delicate in constitution thrive without any difficulty in milder climates, as southern Europe, California, South Africa, and Australia. Cold winds and dampness are the chief enemies of birds in outdoor aviaries, not mere low temperatures.

The most difficult foreign seed eaters to acclimatize are the smaller finches, particularly waxbills from West Africa and Australian finches. These birds are generally imported during the winter months, and when first purchased they should be put into a roomy box-type cage (not an open-wire one), and placed in a room where a temperature of about seventy degrees or higher can be maintained. If the birds seem all right after a day or two, the temperature can be very gradually reduced to about sixty degrees.

This large nest hammock is inhabited by several pairs of birds. Grass is packed in large wire mesh and suspended from the ceiling. The nests are lined with feathers and commercial nesting material. Photographed in Carl Papp's aviaries.

Warmth is most necessary at night. In summer, birds freshly imported from the tropics should be given an opportunity to bask in the sunshine, as sun is a great tonic to small tropical birds, especially those from Australia.

Birds are better and happier in an outdoor aviary in summer, besides being much less trouble to their owner when so housed.

Breeding Foreign Finches

The beginner does not really know the joys of aviculture until he has bred some birds for himself. The fancier who successfully rears a few fine young birds in his first season is quickly fired with ambition to do greater things, and the succeeding season may find him trying his skill with more difficult species.

A large flight cage for finches. This cage is on rollers so that it can easily be moved and is therefore for patio or birdroom.

Double breeding cages and materials used for breeding canaries and larger finches.

Take care that you always have twice as many nest boxes as pairs of birds.

Generally speaking, it is easier to breed finches in outdoor aviaries than in cages. Nevertheless, certain species can be easily bred in large box cages, and among these may be mentioned Cutthroats, Saffron Finches, Bengalese, Silverbills, White Java Sparrows, Gouldian Finches, and Zebra Finches.

There are three items which make for success in foreign bird breeding. The initial stock must be of good stamina and fertility, the accommodation provided must be suitable, and the birds must be properly fed and managed.

A common fault with beginners is that of overcrowding the aviary. Where breeding results are especially desired the number of pairs must be strictly limited. For instance, a small aviary measuring eight feet long by four feet wide should not contain more than half a dozen pairs of small finches for breeding purposes. Overcrowding during breeding operations only results in squabbling and fighting, and the stronger birds will soon develop into bullies and make life miserable for their weaker companions.

27

Nests will be pulled to pieces as soon as they are built, and even if young are hatched under these trying conditions any special food provided for them will be quickly eaten by the stronger birds, and those with families will not have a fair chance of getting their share.

Foreign finches often molt at irregular seasons, and it is quite useless to breed from half-molted birds. Every prospecive pair of breeding birds should be in the best of health and plumage.

Finches prefer natural nesting materials.

Facilities for nesting should be withheld until all birds are fit for the show bench. It needs some restraint on the part of the fancier when summer has arrived and the birds are not yet fully feathered. But if allowed to go to nest in this condition there is a risk of losing some hens from egg-binding, and even if any eggs are laid they will quite likely be infertile.

In small aviaries, most foreign finches will take to box-type nesting boxes, with the front left open for about three inches at the top, or a hole cut for entrance. Hollow logs can be used, or cylinders of wire netting. Put up plenty of nesting boxes, two to each pair of birds if you can find room for them. These should be placed high up near the roof of the aviary, as birds are less inclined to use nest boxes placed low down. If nest boxes are placed in the open flight, they must be under some sort of top cover as protection against heavy rains.

Many finches feed their young on partly digested seeds regurgitated from the crop, but others—as the waxbills and buntings— must have insect fare for the successful rearing of their chicks. Most fanciers offer a little soaked bread or biscuit, or moistened insectile food, to their breeding finches. Be sure that this is not left in the aviary to go stale.

Particular attention should be paid to the feeding of birds during the breeding season. Plenty of natural food is what they most require, and as far as finches are concerned this should consist of seeding grasses, chickweed and groundsel. Seeding heads of dock, shepherd's purse, dandelion and other common weeds of cultivation and pasture lands are mostly appreciated by the typical finches, the weaver finches not caring much about them. It is a good plan to get your finch stock used to eating a little soft food as soon as possible after they are installed in your aviary or bird-room, and before they have any chicks to feed. The birds may hardly taste this at first, but eventually many of them will gladly avail themselves of it to feed their young ones. The same applies to insect food. Some finches will not tackle gentles at first sight, but when they see other birds eating them, they follow suit. A few meal worms are a good tonic to any finch that will eat them.

Soaked seed is a very valuable food, and many finches will rear sound young ones on this alone. Soak some millet or *Panicum* for

Large finch cage used for at least three pairs of finches. Anything less than three pairs in such a cage will result in fighting among the birds.

about three days until it begins to swell and sprout. It will do this at any temperature above fifty degrees.

The fancier should not interfere too much with the nests when birds are breeding, though many kinds do not appear to object to this, provided it is done while the birds are off the nest. Others are extremely shy and will dart off at the slightest disturbance.

A rather critical period is when the young birds leave the nest for the first time. They are then very nervous and may cling to the wires, where cats might attack them. In most cases, the parents are able to get the youngsters back into the nest for the night after their first precarious trip to the outside world. There is generally no need to catch them up unless they are out in bad weather or have got into some dangerous place or situation from which it is obviously impossible for them to extricate themselves.

The period of incubation with the majority of foreign finches is twelve to fourteen days, and the chicks leave the nest about fifteen days after hatching. The young birds should be left with their parents for a week or so until they appear to be feeding themselves satisfactorily, when it is best to separate them. Do this as soon as possible, but make allowances for backward individuals. If left too long with their parents the young birds annoy them by pestering to be fed when they can perfectly well feed themselves. They also prevent the old birds going to nest and bringing up another brood, most foreign finches being willing to rear several broods a season.

Breeding British Finches

Very little interest was shown in the breeding of British finches prior to 1934, when the "Buckmaster Bill" became law in Britain. This prohibited the sale of wild birds unless closed banded. In September of that year the British Bird Breeder's Association was formed to encourage this fascinating branch of aviculture. The Association, after hundreds of tests and experiments, issued bands of the correct sizes, which can only be put on birds in the nestling stage, and which will not become too tight when the bird grows to full size. The rings are differently colored for each year, and bear code numbers. During the first five years of its existence, members of the B.B.B.A. reared to maturity the following species of British finches: Goldfinch, Bullfinch, Greenfinch, Bramble-finch, Hawfinch, Linnet, Siskin, Twite, Redpoll, Chaffinch, Yellow-hammer, Reed Bunting and House Sparrow (normal and white varieties).

The ideal way to breed British finches is to have a number of small aviaries in which a single pair of each species can be housed. Those fanciers who have a small range of compartment aviaries, such as budgerigar breeders use, could wish for nothing better in the way of accommodation. They can, however, be bred in a mixed collection, and some fanciers have been successful in cage-breeding these finches. For a pair of finches a larger type of cage than the ordinary canary double-breeder is advisable, and it should be deeper from front to back.

British finches don't normally take to enclosed box-type nesting boxes. Ordinary canary nest-pans should be hung up out of reach of mice (not on the wire netting), and screened with bunches of

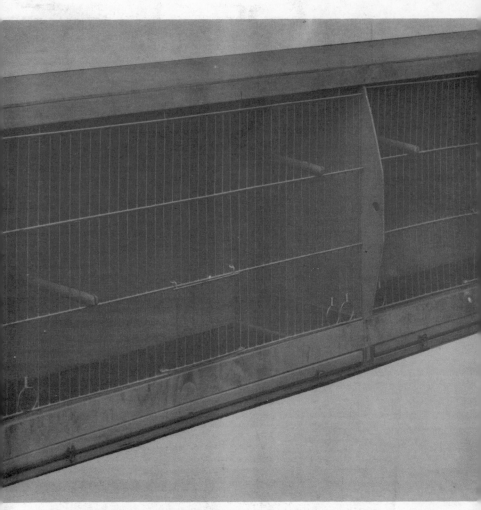

Double breeding cage, usually used for canaries and Zebra Finches.

Opposite:

Red-crested Cardinal. This hardy South American bird measures approximately 7½ inches in length. It is a lively bird but is apt to be aggressive. For this reason, it is suggested that a pair be kept separately or with somewhat larger birds able to defend themselves.

heather or brushwood twigs. Another good idea for the aviary shelter is to erect a shelf of wire netting near the roof and fill up the space with twiggy branches. In any case, the nesting sites should be fixed up early in the year so that the birds have time to get used to them. Do not be sparing in using natural cover to screen the nesting sites of British birds, as they are rarely willing to go to nest in an open situation, as a canary will.

Suitable nesting materials must be provided; sphagnum moss and lichens obtained from country hedgebanks are most useful, as also are any bits of wool, feathers, and similar soft substances which the birds can use as a lining material. Rope or coarse string cut into lengths of about three inches is also much appreciated.

Care must be exercised in selecting the breeding pairs for a mixed collection. Bramblefinch and Chaffinch cocks will usually fight each other. Greenfinches and Crossbills do not get on very well together, neither do Siskins and Redpolls, but birds of either group do not as a rule molest those of the other group. It is the association of nearly related birds that one must guard against.

If you wish to breed Chaffinches or Bramblefinches, remember that these two species feed their young on insect fare. Goldfinches and Hawfinches feed their nestlings on partly digested food regurgitated from the crop. Bullfinches require plenty of berries in their diet.

II Food

Aviculturists divide birds into three main classes, according to the nature of their diet. These are the seed- and grain-eating birds, or hardbills, as they are popularly termed; the insectivorous birds, or soft-bills; and the nectar-feeding birds, which in a state of nature live largely on honey and nectar sipped from flowers.

These divisions are not really so well-defined as they may at first appear, for few birds are so rigidly restricted in their choice of food, and some kinds are omnivorous. Many finches, which are generally regarded as seed-eating birds, also consume a number of insects, and some kinds feed their young largely on them.

Nearly all finches, too, are fond of green food, and in captivity this is an essential item in their diet. Because of the ease with which seed-eating species are fed and manged, they are deservedly the most popular of cage and aviary birds. But the fancier should not overlook the need for variety in fare essential for the well-being of even this class of birds.

We have still a lot to discover about the exact food requirements of birds in captivity, but it has been found that a more varied diet is necessary for maintaining birds in health and condition than was formerly thought adequate. Many finches are remarkably tough in constitution and can survive for a long time on what appears to a dietician to be unsuitable fare, but the genuine fancier whose aim is to keep his pets healthy and contented for the full term of their natural lives will seek to give them a well-balanced diet.

On an unbalanced diet, such as a single kind of seed or even a mixture of seeds and nothing else, no species of bird could maintain perfect health for long. Its condition would vary from day to day, gradually getting worse, till serious disease resulted after a brave struggle between the malnourished body and the forces of degeneration. Experiments have proved that even when a bird is given canary seed only—and this is by far the most valuable seed as bird food—it is insufficient to supply all physiological needs, just as is any other unbalanced diet.

Red-headed Finch. The sexes of this species are easy to distinguish, but they are practically impossible to breed in an aviary with other birds as they are quite easily disturbed. Their importation from South Africa has recently been limited.

Cordon Bleu. Even though this bird is reputedly delicate and susceptible to damage by sudden major changes in temperature and wet weather, once it is acclimatized it can live for quite a few years. Some Cordon Bleus have lasted up to 14 years. They nest readily but are easier to breed in an indoor aviary.

Pintailed Nonpareil. This is a difficult bird to rear successfully, as they are rather delicate. They require plenty of space to exercise, or else they will sit motionless and become overweight and ill. They are usually kept only by experienced fanciers. The orange blotch on the underparts of this species (only the male has the blotch) is shown in the photo below; the grass-green color of the wings is shown at right.

Vitamins (left) are essential during breeding. Natural lava stone helps keep the bird's beak trimmed and healthy.

It may be argued that in a state of nature birds are sometimes compelled to feed on one kind of seed for a certain period. But in the great majority of cases this only occurs for short intervals of time and rarely persists for more than one season of the year. It is the nature of wild birds to consume a variety of foodstuffs, and the best results will follow by imitating this in captivity. It is the practice of all experienced fanciers to feed their hard-billed birds on a stock mixture of seeds for convenience, but to also give wild seeds and green food when these are available.

Proteins and Carbohydrates

The food requirements of birds are not always the same. Anyone who has studied our wild birds will know how different their diet is in winter from that in summer. Breeding birds require an abundance of every essential food element, while young birds need a food rich in good protein especially, but not much energy food, because they do not in the nestling stage exert much energy. Birds which are neither breeding nor molting, on the other hand, require a diet poor in protein but rich in carbohydrate, as they spend most of the time flying about. For breeding birds, quality in protein is more important than quantity. Insects, ant eggs, cheese, hard-boiled egg, and green food all contain protein of high biological value, while seeds are very poor in it. Soya bean, which is sometimes used as an ingredient of bird foods, is, however, an exception.

In cold weather, birds require more carbohydrate, since this is the chief promoter of bodily heat. Protein also produces warmth, but it is not ideal for the purpose because the large quantities necessary would compel the bird's body to assimilate more uric acid than it could excrete. Any such undue accumulation of acid would, of course, lead to lowered health and eventual disease.

Another factor to be taken into consideration is whether or not a food is palatable. It is not enough to say that such-and-such a seed represents good feeding value. This may be so, but it is quite useless if the fancier cannot get his birds to eat it. Birds are often annoyingly conservative in their likes and dislikes. This is especially the case with the foreign finches—waxbills, grass-finches, mannikins and the like—which will rarely eat any seeds other than canary, millet, and grass seeds. Which seeds are palatable, and which less favored, can only be ascertained by actual feeding tests in which the birds are allowed to take their choice of different seeds. Though it is the usual practice to supply birds with a mixture of seeds, it is probably better to supply the chief seeds in separate containers and allow the birds free choice. Then, if it is desired to give some of the very palatable, but high-priced seeds, or especially fattening kinds, or seeds rich in proteins at nesting time, limited quantities of these can be mixed with any one of the main seeds, or given in separate vessels.

Soaked Seed

It is well known among experienced fanciers that the feeding value of live seeds is greater than that of old seeds in which the germ is dead. This is due to the fact that certain of the vitamins so essential to the healthy development of birds disappear from seeds after they have been kept too long. All birds benefit from being given some sprouted seed now and again. All that is necessary is to soak the seed for a few hours and then spread it on a damp cloth.

Java Rice Bird. Although these birds can be a disturbing element among other small birds, it is recommended that one pair be kept with other birds of the same size for breeding purposes. If left to themselves, pairs can be rather slow to nest and some can even take years. When they are attempting to rear a family, they should be provided with artificial light till about 9 p.m. and again at about 7 a.m. to alleviate the darkness they are not accustomed to.

Golden-Breasted Waxbill. The "song" of this West African bird is a rather monotonous chirping sound which lasts from early morning until late at night. It is a small bird, measuring only 3½-3¾ inches in length.

Red-billed Weaver. This frequently imported, industrious African bird will begin construction of a nest almost immediately upon placement in an aviary. They are always busy and will often destroy one nest in order to start another. They are colony nesters.

Wheat germ oil is a natural aid in keeping plumage and skin healthy and conditioned. Ask at your pet store for dosage and other benefits.

If kept in a warm place the seed, if alive, will start to sprout, and in this condition is much liked by birds.

When birds have young to feed they will also appreciate soaked seed. The seed should be covered with water and allowed to stand for about a day. Pour off the water, rinse the seed in a fresh supply, and again strain off the water. The seed is then ready to be given to the birds.

Here are the principal nutrients found in some of the seeds commonly used as food for cage birds—**canary:** water, 7.0; protein, 14; fat, 5.8; carbohydrates, 55; starch equivalent, 72.6; nutrient ratio, 1 to 5.3. **Millet:** water, 7.0; crude protein, 12.6; fat, 4.2; carbohydrates, 64.4; starch equivalent, 63.5; nutrient ratio, 1 to 6.2. **Rape:** water, 7.0; crude protein, 19; fat, 40; carbohydrates, 10; starch equivalent, 131.3; nutrient ratio, 1 to 7.7. **Oatmeal:** water, 7.0; crude protein, 11; fat, 5; carbohydrates, 56.3; starch equivalent, 69.2; nutrient ratio, 1 to 4.6.

With the exception of maw and sesame, all seeds are deficient in lime, sodium, chlorine, and vitamins A and D. Iodine may or may not be represented, this depending upon the soil in which the seed was grown. All seeds contain sufficient phosphorous for the needs of birds. Linseed contains appreciable quantities of vitamins A and D, but this is but little used as a bird food. To insure adequate vitamins, birds should be given a regular supply of green food, as it is in this form that they are most readily assimilable.

Salt and Lime

Sodium and chlorine may be supplied in the form of ordinary table salt, or when obtainable, evaporated sea water, which also contains some iodine and other valuable minerals. In either case only minute quantities are required—about a level teaspoonful to a pint of water. When practicable, the safest way of supplying salt to birds is to add sea water to the drinking water at the rate of one pint sea water to ten of pure water, which brings the salt content of the latter up to about a third of one percent.

Cuttlefish bone is a natural source of calcium and chlorine, both of which are essential for the health of your finches.

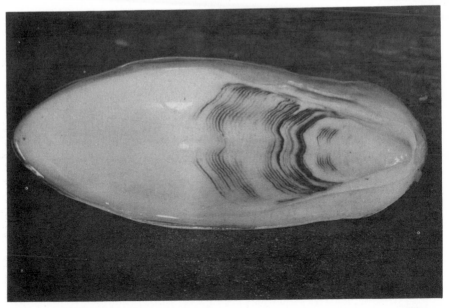

Rainbow Bunting. This native American bird is easily tamed and can be kept with other birds in a well-planted outside flight in summer. During the winter, however, they should be housed in a frost-free bird room. They are not as frequently available as the Nonpareil Bunting, and breeding success in captivity is not yet recorded.

Star Finch. These birds are usually seen in pairs in the wild, and only during the breeding period or a particularly dry spell will they congregate in small groups near a waterhole. Although they are generally regarded as hardy birds, they thrive on direct sunlight and should be provided with heat during the winter.

Cutthroat Finch. This robust little bird derives its name from the bright red slash of color across the throat of the male. They will thrive for years and can be kept in an outside flight. They should, however, remain undisturbed during breeding attempts.

Salt greatly increases the ferility of birds, for which reason plenty of lime must be present to supply the shell for the eggs produced. Salt is not good for birds if they do not have it in conjunction with lime, and this fact should always be borne in mind.

Perhaps the best form in which to supply lime to birds is as oystershell grit, which is almost one hundred percent calcium carbonate. This also contains sufficient iodine for the well-being of birds. Cuttlefish bone contains about eighty percent of lime, and this is present in a readily digestible form. It is, however, not much use hanging up a piece of cuttlebone for birds to pick at, as it is too hard for them in most cases and they are unable to obtain a sufficient supply. Instead, it should be pulverized and mixed with soft food or ground into small pieces which the birds can pick up easily.

Green Food

The main value of green food is in preventing excess uric acid formation, which is the natural result of a diet consisting of dry seeds. Without a supply of green food birds are liable to such diseases as nephritis, pericarditis, and gouty affections, caused by acid conditions of the system. These acid producing tendencies in the staple diet of seed-eating birds should be counteracted by the natural alkalis to be found in green food and in vegetable juices.

An excellent form of green food for birds is chickweed. This ubiquitous plant is easily recognized by its tiny white starry flowers and small, succulent, pale green leaves. It grows abundantly on allotments and cultivated places where the soil is rich. It wilts quickly when gathered, but will soon pick up again if the stalks are placed in water for a while. It can be tied up in bunches and fastened to the wires of the cage, or fixed in special holders sold for the purpose.

Chickweed can be found on rich, cultivated land throughout the year in temperate climes, and almost any species of finch will eat it with beneficial results. The green leaves and shoots of chickweed contain vital elements essential to the good health of your birds. Breeding pairs should have fresh chickweed daily.

Groundsel is another excellent green food. It has small yellow flowers without petals, like tiny dandelions, which are followed by feathery tufts of seed vessels. Birds will eat both the leaves and flowers. Shepherd's purse, watercress, and lettuce are all equally valuable green foods. Dandelion is especially valuable, and is looked upon by fanciers as a tonic food. The whole plant should be lifted and offered to the birds. Green food should not be given to birds in a wet or frosted condition.

In the summer and autumn, wild seeds should be gathered as a tonic and diet change for finches. British finches, and all typical finches, greatly appreciate these. One of the most readily collected is dock. One can strip off handfuls of the seeds with ease. The brown, triangular-shaped seeds are rich in oil and its regular use imparts a fine sheen to the plumage of British finches. In season it can be fed to the birds by simply breaking off the seeding heads.

Seed heads of dandelion, knapweed, thistles, and hawkweeds should be gathered before they open. These should be spread to dry on a tray, the bottom of which is made of perforated zinc. Stand this over a shallow box containing a lining of newspaper. When the heads open rub them over the tray, and the seeds will fall through the perforations and can be gathered up in the newspaper.

Seeding heads of grasses are best gathered and tied up in bunches and hung up in a shed to dry. The seeds will remain on the stalks if treated in this way, and can be supplied to the birds in winter. Many other plants, as persicaria, seeding heads of lettuce, shepherd's purse, and other weeds of pasture and neglected farmland can be collected in autumn and hung up to dry in paper bags. The seed will then drop out. Some garden flowers in the seed state are appreciated by finches, such as cornflowers, mignonette, sunflower, etc.

It is important to choose dry conditions for collecting seeds which are to be stored for winter use. If gathered when wet they will go musty with mildew. Where fairly large quantities are needed, they will store well in sacks hung up in a dry garden shed or cellar.

1. Gouldian Finch (Red-headed); 2. Three-colored Mannikin;
3. Paradise Whydah; 4. Orange-cheeked Waxbill; 5. Long-tailed
Grass-Finch; 6. Java Sparrow; 7. Avadavat; 8. Cutthroat Finch.

9. Grey Waxbill; 10. Napoleon Weaver; 11. Pintail Whydah;
12. Zebra Finch; 13. Lavender Finch; 14. Orange Bishop; 15. Cordon Bleu; 16. African Fire-finch.

III Keeping Birds Healthy

Birds are not easy creatures to cure when they fall sick, and some precautions are necessary if their well-being is to be maintained.*

One of the chief causes of ailments among foreign finches is fluctuating temperatures. Many birds from warm climates can withstand cold remarkably well; but a sudden drop in temperature, even in the height of summer, can start troublesome chills. Both in the bird-room and outdoor aviary every precaution against drafts, damp, excessive heat or cold should be taken.

Cleanliness is also very important. Disease can be rapidly spread through drinking water being allowed to remain contaminated with birds' droppings. Fresh water daily should be the rule in the aviary, and it may be necessary to renew the supplies more frequently in the case of birds in cages.

Wing exercise, especially during the winter months, is essential to the health of birds, particularly those kept caged indoors. See that your cages have a good length, as this is more important than depth or height.

Always keep the floor of the cages clean and covered with sand, on which cage bird grit is sprinkled. Remove all the stale green food or soft food at the end of the day. Do not give birds wet or frosted green food.

In spite of all precautions birds will sometimes fall ill. The usual symptom is fluffed-out plumage—though this may be merely because the bird is feeling cold. The fancier soon learns to detect signs of trouble among his birds, and the important thing is to act at once. It is no use leaving a bird which seems poorly among its companions. Neither will a sick bird which has eggs or young be any help to its mate. There is only one rule with ailing birds—remove them to a hospital cage.

---

*Consult: *Bird Diseases* by L. Arnall and I.F. Keymer (TFH Publications, Inc., Neptune, N.J.)

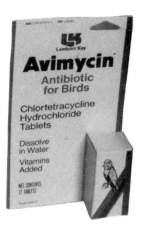

Formulated to combat specific illnesses common to captive finches and other birds, health aids can be purchased at your pet store.

When trimming nails, never cut too close; you may cut into the veins, causing bleeding.

Zebra Finch. This is the most popular of all the Australian finches. The Zebra Finch can be obtained in many colors and is available almost everywhere.

Melba Finch. Only experienced fanciers should attempt to keep these delicate South African birds, as their acclimatization is difficult and requires much attention. For the first few weeks after their arrival the birds should be kept in a warm, sunny location. The male Melba Finch shown in the photo below shows an abnormally heavy concentration of red on the throat. The Melba Finches shown above are more typical of the species.

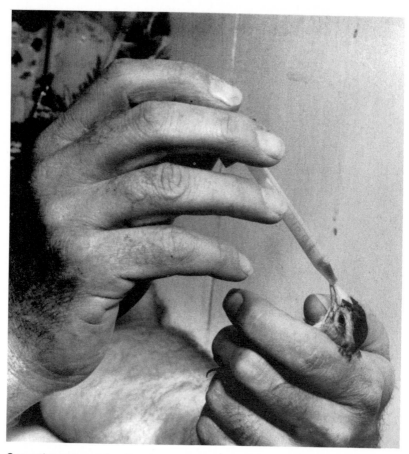

Sometimes hand feeding is necessary, as in the case of a sick bird that will not eat or in the administration of medicine.

Every fancier should have such a cage. Excellent types fitted with thermostatically controlled heaters are on the market, and one cannot do better than secure one of these. A simple but quite useful hospital cage can be made out of ordinary grocer's boxes. This should have a glass front, made to slip up and down, and have a false metal floor. Under this is a heating element in the form of two or more forty-watt electric bulbs. It is best to have these arranged so that they can be switched on independently, so that one can control the amount of heat required. A cage should be fitted with a perch, not too high up, as well as with a small food and water container. The cage should have a thermometer hung on the back wall where it can be easily read.

Heat is a prime necessity in curing sick birds. It is the only cure in most cases, and certainly one cannot do anything without it in the treatment of an egg-bound hen. Sometimes birds, especially young ones which appear almost at the last gasp from exposure, will revive if placed in the hospital cage at a temperature of around eighty degrees or so.

All medicine should be given in water, in either glass or porcelain drinkers, never in metal ones.

Accidents

One of the commonest accidents among birds is their habit of flying against glass window panes. This is mostly the case with pet birds allowed to fly about a dwelling room. In the aviary and bird-room all glass lights should be covered with half-inch wire netting. Birds will dash against glass substitutes when frightened, but we have personally not had any injured in this way, as the substitutes "give" more easily and, of course, do not splinter if broken.

Broken legs sometimes occur from a bird having become caught by its claws in some portion of the wirework or fittings. If the break is at a joint, little can be done, and the leg will always remain stiff. But, if broken off at the shank bone, the injured limb may be set with the aid of splints. These should be cut from small strips of wood and made as light as possible. The splints should extend from the foot well up the thigh, but see that the upper ends are not long enough to injure the body of the bird during movement. Wrap the splints lightly in cottonwool and place them in position. Bind them firmly, but not too tightly, with a continuous wrapping of narrow, soft tape. Birds' bones knit very quickly, and the best way to be sure it is time to remove the dressing is to watch the movements of the patient. When the bird appears to be perching well and gripping the support with the toes in a natural manner, the splints may be removed. Some stiffness of the limb remains for a while, but this will right itself eventually. A badly damaged broken leg in which the skin is torn and twisted should be amputated with a pair of sharp scissors. The stump soon heals.

Scaly-crowned Weaver. These birds are rather delicate and acclimatization must be gradual. They breed in colonies, but fully successful breeding results in captivity are rare.

Chaffinch. The most common of all European finches, the Chaffinch is easily distinguished by the combination of white shoulder-patch, white wing-bar, and white in tail. It is an extremely robust bird.

Senegal Combassou. Like the Paradise Whydah, this bird also has plumage that changes during breeding time, although only in color. The species has been known to breed in captivity, but success is rare.

Serin. This form of wild canary originates in southern Europe. They breed readily and can be crossed with the domestic canary.

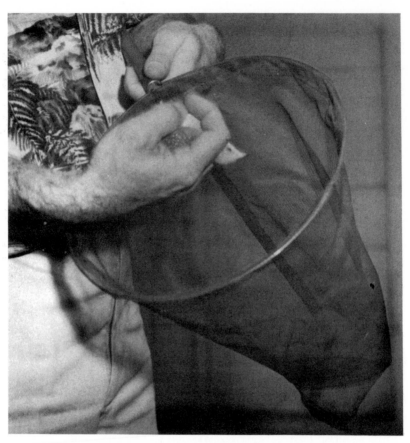

Nets used for catching birds should not have very open meshing, as the claws of the birds can catch in the large openings.

Broken wings must be set in a natural position. Do not try to use splints. Instead, the two wings are bound to the body with a narrow tape dressing until the break has healed. This takes about ten days.

Apoplexy

This is often the cause of sudden death, and the bird may die too quickly for any form of treatment. Birds kept in too small cages, overfed and allowed insufficient exercise, are most subject to this complaint. When an attack comes on, the victim becomes dizzy, and falls to the ground with convulsed limbs. If one can get at the bird before it expires, and plunge its head into a dish of water, it may recover. The patient should then be caged on its own and kept perfectly quiet for a few days.

Asthma

The symptoms of this are coughing, tightness of breathing, and weakness. Small doses of potassium bromide may be administered by the beak.

Bare of Feathers

Some finches, particularly waxbills, frequently lose their feathers, especially those of the head. This is common in newly imported birds, and can usually be cured by turning the birds into an oudoor aviary, where they will receive direct sunshine. In winter, this is not possible, but the addition to the drinking water of a little orange juice may effect a cure. The cause is generally too much rich, oily seeds which overload the system with food poisons, causing damage to the cell capillaries of the skin. Plenty of green food, especially dandelion and spinach, will put matters right.

Bird fanciers should be especially attentive to the problem of eradicating parasites from their birds' living quarters. Ask your pet dealer for advice about safe and effective anti-parasite products.

Hooded Siskin. These charming birds can be kept together in a large aviary, but quarrels will break out during breeding periods. Canary breeders have crossed the Hooded Siskin with regular canaries to obtain an orange to orange-red canary.

Dusky Twinspot. A rare bird, the Dusky Twinspot was imported into Europe for the first time in 1963. No success in breeding in captivity has been attained as of yet.

European Siskin. Bird fanciers have found this bird easy to tame and a pleasant addition to cage or aviary. They breed well, even in a large cage, as long as they have a well camouflaged nest box.

Wing clipping—used to tame wild birds—is performed on one wing only, always leaving the first three or four feathers untouched.

Bare patches are also sometimes due to birds plucking each other. Some birds develop this vice when overcrowded, as when being imported, but give it up when turned into an aviary where they have other diversions. However, offenders should be removed from other birds, if it is intended to keep them in cages, and caged by themselves.

Bronchitis

This is caused by inflammation of the bronchial tubes. The affected bird shows signs of weakness and labored breathing accompanied by a wheezing, rasping noise. Bad ventilation, exposure to damp and cold, and sudden changes in temperature are all causes of this complaint.

A mixture generally effective is glycerine, oxymel of squills, and ipecac wine in equal quantities. Give half a teaspoonful of the mixture to three teaspoonsful of drinking water.

Chills

Birds get colds and chills in the same way as do humans—by drafts and sudden changes in temperature. They are more subject to the complaint if their resistance is in any way lowered. In winter, for instance, the long nights and short hours of daylight do not enable many tropical species to take sufficient food. Artificial lighting in the aviary and bird-room will enable this trouble to be overcome. A bird suffering from a chill sits puffed up, often with shivering wings. There may be running from the nostrils. Heat is the main remedy. The bird should be placed in the hospital cage at a temperature of not less than eighty degrees Fahrenheit for a few hours. If the bird seems to be less distressed, the temperature may be gradually lowered. Birds brought inside from outdoor quarters in winter suffering from chills should not be put outside again until spring.

Coccidiosis

This is a parasitic disease of the intestine, which sets up inflammation or enteritis. It runs a rapid course, killing in two or three days. The symptoms are fluffed out plumage, restlessness, and sometimes diarrhea. Death generally takes place during an attack of convulsions. The corpse is usually emaciated. The disease is most prevalent in early summer and is contagious. Cages in which birds known to be suffering from coccidiosis have been kept should be thoroughly cleaned with boiling water containing caustic soda. It is better to go over them with a blow-lamp. Tincture of catechu should be given in the drinking water, about five drops in every teaspoonful of water. It should be continued for several days.

Constipation

This is not uncommon trouble among birds. The chief symptom is a frequent attempt to evacuate without results. A good old remedy is to add ten drops of syrup of buckthorn to a drinker of

Gouldian Finch. These Australian finches are rather difficult to acclimatize. Even a bird which looks healthy may suddenly die in the cage. Once acclimatized, however, they become quite hardy and can even survive the winter in an unheated room.

Paradise Whydah. Ordinarily the male of this species is a dull beige bird measuring 5½ inches in length. At breeding time, however, it is transformed into a 20-inch-long gaudy cock. The two center tail feathers grow to more than 10 inches in length. For this reason a large cage, or preferably a bird room, is required.

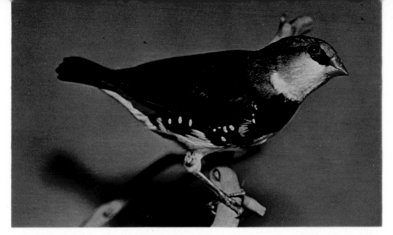

Diamond Sparrow. Although this species is quite easily bred, they can become quite fat and unfit for breeding unless kept in a roomy aviary. The sexes are rather difficult to distinguish. Sudden changes in temperature could prove fatal.

Nonpareil Bunting. Of all species of finches, this is the most easily bred and one of the most tame. The cock will attain full color by the spring of the year.

water. A very small pinch of Glauber's salts to the drinking water is also recommended. Birds suffering from constipation should be encouraged to eat green food, seeding grasses, and millet seed soaked until it begins to sprout.

Diarrhea

There are very many possible causes of diarrhea or enteritis, and it can be in a mild form or serious to a fatal degree. Diarrhea may be set up by viruses, decomposed foods, poisonous plants, bacteria, protozoa, etc. Chills may predispose birds to develop the complaint. It can also be readily brought on in birds from fright in catching them, or by sudden changes in food. Young, immature, and freshly acquired birds are more liable to it. Stale egg food is a sure and deadly cause of enteritis. Dirty or infected cages, food and water vessels, moldly or dusty seed are all possible causes of the trouble. Sudden climatic changes will often bring on an attack of diarrhea in tropical finches, as it lowers the resistance of the birds. Lack of suitable grit is a common cause of diarrhea from digestive troubles.

Birds suffering from the trouble have the undertail feathers soiled, and their droppings may be watery. Sufferers should be kept warm, and warmth alone often brings a bird round. A few drops of chlorodyne in the drinking water is the safest medicine to give.

 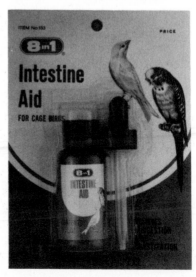

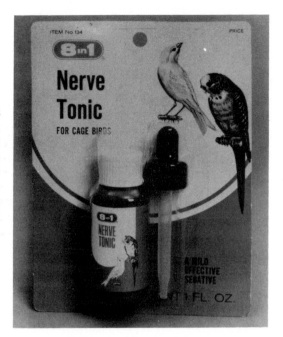

Tonics and preventives such as the ones pictured here and on the opposite page may be purchased at any pet shop dealing in birds and bird supplies.

Egg-binding

This is easily the most troublesome ailment of the breeding aviary, and probably more hen birds are lost through it than any other cause. Egg-binding is really a cramp of the oviduct, and occurs during wet, chilly weather most frequently. The bird invariably leaves her nest and sits on the floor fluffed-up and in pain. She can seldom fly more than a few feet, and may crouch in a corner. Heat is the only cure. If the bird is gently caught up and placed in a box before a fire or, better still, in a hospital cage heated to about eighty-five or ninety degrees Fahrenheit, the chances are she will quickly recover. The egg should be laid within a few hours, and the bird must not be returned to her cage or aviary until this has taken place. She will rarely take any further interest in sitting for some weeks. Some fanciers make a practice of anointing the vent with olive oil, using a camel-hair paint brush for the purpose. Others believe in holding the bird over a jug of boiling water. But the writers have had very satisfactory results simply by putting the birds in a cage, and maintaining a steady heat. Give seed and water, as the bird will take this as soon as the pain from the cramp is relieved by the warmth.

Chestnut-breasted Finch. These birds will be better off in a fairly large aviary, as they tend to get fat and listless in a cage. They are difficult to sex, the song of the male being the only sure indication. They are a hardy bird and can spend the winter in an unheated aviary with an adequate shelter.

Green Cardinal. A native of Brazil and Paraguay, this bird has proved strong enough to withstand the winter in an outside flight. Although they are aggressive during the breeding season, at other times (or when only one cock is kept) they can be housed with several other birds.

Mexican Cardinal. A subspecies of the Virginian Cardinal, this bird, like other cardinals, is aggressive during breeding season and should be housed separately if nesting is desired. Live food is required for a healthy brood.

Sometimes a hen is egg-bound with the first egg of her second clutch, though it is generally the first egg of the season which causes the trouble. A hen may be prone to egg-binding, and should be constantly watched when laying. Some species are more prone to the trouble than others. Cut-throats, otherwise very hardy birds, are liable to egg-binding in inclement weather. One cause of egg-binding is the lack of a shell on the egg, in which case the muscles cannot properly expel it. See that your birds have a plentiful supply of suitable shell grit and cuttlefish bone. Slaked garden lime may be put in their bath and drinking water, especially if your water supply is of the "soft" type.

Parasites

Birds are, unfortunately, subject to many parasites. As far as cage and aviary specimens are concerned, only mites are likely to be a source of trouble. Of these, red mites are the most troublesome pest. These mites suck the blood of the birds at night, leaving their victims in the daytime and hiding in cracks in the woodwork. They are often found in the slits at the ends of the perches, or, in metal ornamental cages, they collect in the metal dome at the top of the cage. A metal cage can be rid of these mites with the aid of boiling water. Wood cages and nest boxes should be treated with liquid household disinfectant. If a dark color is not objected to, there is nothing better than creosote for keeping red mites in check.

Feather mites live on the birds and do not regularly leave their hosts as do red mites. They are tiny grayish creatures which irritate the birds and in bad cases cause ragged plumage. Treatment consists of dusting the plumage of affected birds with insect powder, a safe kind being derris dust, as used by gardeners. Or you can use flowers of sulphur.

IV True Finches

The true Finches (*Fringillinae*) are among the most popular of all cage birds and include all the British species. Their main attraction is that they are hardy, easily maintained in either cage or aviary, while many are pleasing songsters. Their diet should be mixed seeds, greenstuff and the seeding heads of various wild plants in season. They build cupshaped nests in thick bushes and low trees, and are good breeders in captivity. All these birds feed their young from the crop, regurgitating swallowed food into the mouths of the chicks. Some of them, however, as buntings, sparrows, chaffinches, and bramblefinches, also give their young insects as caught. Even after the young have left the nest, they are fed by the parents on regurgitated food from time to time.

Chaffinch (*Fringilla coelebs*)

Description: Forehead black; crown and nape blue-gray; back and scapulars, chestnut, tinged green; rump green; breast wine-red, fading to white on the abdomen; wings blackish, with two white bands; tail black, two central feathers gray, the two outer ones on each side black, with a broad oblique white band. The hen is mostly brownish above, grayish white below. The white bands are less distinct. Length: six inches (152.4 mm). Habitat: Europe.

The Chaffinch is said to be the commonest bird in the British Isles, and certainly there are few parts of Britain where the cheerful "pink, pink" call of this lovely finch cannot be heard. Being bright, alert and active, aviary life suits this splendid finch best, though it is commonly kept in a cage and will do well under such conditions provided the cage is reasonably spacious.

It goes to nest readily in an aviary, but the young are not too easy to rear. The probable reason is that the Chaffinch is more insectivorous than other British hard-bills and should have insect fare and soft-bill mixture when rearing young. Chaffinches do not seem to care much about green food, but they are very fond of sprouted seeds, and for the purpose such seeds as rape, turnip, and radish are suitable. The seed mixture should contain canary, rape,

Cuban Finch. Regularly imported into Europe from Cuba, this bird has become fairly popular in the U.S. It is, however, a somewhat hostile bird, especially during breeding season.

Pearl-headed Silverbill. Determination of sex in these birds is difficult at best. The breast of the female is slightly lighter than that of the male and the spots slightly smaller. A more effective method is the study of the nuptial dance of the male, but even this is not always 100% effective.

Red-collared Whydah. This South African bird is rather large, measuring about 14 inches in length, and does well when a pair is given an aviary to themselves.

King's or Pintailed Whydah. Males, when in their ornamental plumage, are rather aggressive and can frighten other birds in the aviary. Given sufficient room, they can be kept together with weavers and Zebra Finches.

hemp, linseed, and maw. In an aviary the cock Chaffinch is liable
to be spiteful toward weaker birds, especially in spring. The song
is a repetition of seven or eight notes. Unlike most birds, the Chaffinch apparently does not pair for life, since large flocks of cock
birds gather together around farmyards in winter.

English fanciers have had the best success in breeding Chaffinches in small flights, about five or six feet in length, about the
same height, and perhaps only two or three feet wide. The only
shelter necessary (in Britain, at any rate) is a shelf of bush
heather, fir branches, etc., with a strip of galvanized iron, fibro-
cement sheet, or like over the top to keep off the heavy rain and
snow. The Chaffinch is a cold climate bird and does not do at all
well in warmer climes. Only a single pair are placed in these
flights. Nesting material supplied should consist of moss, fine dry
grass, tow, and cotton wool. A number of nesting sites should be
put up in spring, as the hen is very choosy about the position in
which she places her nest. The hen sits closely, and the cock
brings her tidbits of food. The eggs hatch in a fortnight. At this
time, gentles, meal worms, aphis, and a mixture of crushed biscuit
and hard-boiled egg should be supplied. Young Chaffinches can
be hand-reared, but it is an extremely difficult task. The Chaffinch
has hybridized with the Bramblefinch and Greenfinch, as well as
with the canary.

For show purposes a Chaffinch should be large and shapely,
standing well up on his perch, but not too long in the leg or showing very much thigh. The head should be neat, with a good, full
eye; a rather prominent chest with a nice curve to the vent; a well-
filled back with the wings tightly braced to the sides, and perfect
wing and tail feathers. The color should be bright and lustrous,
with the cap perfectly blue. The breast must be rich and even in
color, and of a rather deep ruddy hue. Wing markings should be
clear and distinct, the white shoulder patch standing out in strong
contrast to the chestnut of the back.

A few foreign chaffinches have been occasionally imported to
England, but we doubt if they have been seen in the United States.
Among them is the Blue Chaffinch (*F. teydea*) of Tenerife. It is
slate blue, with some white on the wings, and is the largest of its
genus (6½ in. or 165.1 mm) Reputed to be aggressive in disposition, it is confined to a single stretch of pine forest. It is not a good

cage and aviary bird as it remains nervous. The Madeiran Chaffinch (*F. maderensis*) is mostly slate colored above with a fawn chest. It was imported as long ago as 1895, by Mr. Abrahams, who gave a pair to Dr. A.G. Butler. He says, "They struck me as being more confiding than our European species and less excitable. The song was louder and the note of defiance was repeated four or five times, whereas our bird is generally contented with two utterances."

The Algerian Chaffinch (*F. spodiogenys*) is a delightful bird, found in northeast Africa, where it is a popular cage bird. It is very rarely imported, but the London Zoo received specimens as early as 1864.

Brambling (*F. montifringilla*)

Description: Top and sides of the head, upper back, black, the feathers in winter being tipped with brownish; neck and scapulars orange brown; wings black, with orange-brown and white markings; rump and lower parts white; reddish on the flanks, with a few dark spots. The hen is brownish rufous on the crown, feathers tipped with gray; a black streak over the eyes; cheeks and neck ash-gray; all the other colors less bright. Length: six in. (152.4 mm) Habitat: northern Europe and Russia.

The Brambling, or Bramblefinch, is a winter visitor to the British Isles from the north, and is mostly seen in beech woods. It departs about the end of April, before the cocks get their full summer plumage, and does not breed in Britain. In breeding plumage the cocks are very handsome birds with a prominant white rump, chestnut breast and throat, and blue-black mantle. The hen is somewhat like a hen Chaffinch, but more distinctly marked, and has orange patches on the flights and a white one on her lower back, and there is usually some orange on the breast.

Bramblings do not take to captivity as readily as do most finches, and though handsome additions to an aviary they have little to recommend them as cage birds. The cock has only one note in his song—"Zee-e," and is inclined to be spiteful with weaker birds. On the other hand it makes a good exhibition bird, and a show specimen should be large and shapely, with a nice easy carriage. The head and back should be a rich blue-black and well spangled.

Tri-colored Nun. This hardy Indian bird can be kept outside in the winter. It is not yet classed as a free breeder.

Bronze-winged Mannikin. This African bird is not an easy breeder and is consequently more popular for its dramatic markings (glossy black, grey-brown, and snow-white with a spot of greenish bronze in the shoulders). The song of the cock is barely audible, but it is the only certain method by which he can be distinguished from the female.

Masked Finch. The best indication of sex in this species is song, but when two males are housed together, they hardly sing at all. The birds are rather peaceful by nature, but will fight with Long-tailed Grass Finches during the breeding period.

Black-headed / White-headed Mannikins. These species are not very readily bred. However, if breeding is not desired they are a friendly, tolerant addition to any mixed collection.

The Brambling will breed quite readily in an aviary, especially a naturally planted one, where the nest is usually placed in a bush. Several broods are reared during the season, the incubation period being a very brief one of nine days only. The young are largely reared on insects, and so breeding birds should be offered ant eggs, gentles, meal worms, caterpillars, and other garden insects. The Bramblings will hybridize fairly readily with the Chaffinch, but not with other finches.

Goldfinch (*Carduelis carduelis*)

Description: Back of the head, nape and around the base of the beak black; forehead and throat rich crimson; cheeks, forepart of the neck and lower parts white; back dark chestnut brown; wings black with conspicuous yellow and white markings; tail black, tipped with white. Length: five inches (127 mm). Habitat: Europe, Central Asia and North Africa.

Because of its great beauty, cheerful note, and smart appearance, the Goldfinch ranks very high indeed in the estimation of fanciers. The sexes are much alike, but the hen is slightly smaller than the cock. Her beak is not quite so straight, the crimson blaze on the face is narrower, the rump distinctly browner, wing browner, and the yellow band across the wing is narrower and a paler yellow in adult birds. Young birds have a gray head and are called "graypates" by English fanciers.

The Goldfinch is a good breeder in an aviary, and will sometimes nest successfully in a large cage. Breeding birds should be encouraged to eat a little soft food, either canary rearing food, or bread and milk. A simple way to get the birds to take this is to sprinkle some seed on the soft food. When they pick out the seed they taste the soft food and from then on they will usually accept it. Goldfinches as a rule go to nest rather later in the season than other British species.

A good seed mixture for Goldfinches consists of four parts teazle, three parts canary, two parts hemp, one part linseed and one-half part summer rape. Most individuals are fond of hemp seed and some fanciers give this separately, which is quite a good plan. In addition to this a special mixture of choice seeds can be offered as a change, this consisting of one-half pint of niger, two

The Goldfinch is an amicable bird and is easily bred in the proper environment.

Long-tailed or Shafttail Finch. Although the importation of this beautiful Australian bird is now prohibited, there has been a sufficient amount reared in Europe to make it possible—but expensive—to obtain them. They become extremely aggressive during breeding season and have been known to kill small finches. They are fairly hardy and can be housed in an unheated room during the winter.

Greenfinch. A tenacious singer, the Greenfinch will sometimes sing for hours at a time. At the end of the song-burst it emits a long, drawn-out wheeze which can be tire-some. This bird is a reliable breeder, although it has been noted that approx-imately 40% of the young will die inex-plicably around the time of the moult. No reasons have yet been offered for this strange occurrence.

European Goldfinch. It is possible to keep several Goldfinches together in a large aviary with other birds of the same size, but it is best to provide a separate aviary for breeding. It has been a favorite among fanciers for many years.

ounces each of thistle, dandelion, gold of pleasure, and sesame, with one-half pint of maw seed. A spoonful of this mixture per bird can be given every other day. Plenty of green food should be offered, especially watercress, dandelion and seeding grass. Goldfinches are also rather fond of cracked sunflower seeds.

The Goldfinch is an excellent exhibition bird, but since classes for it are usually well filled, it is necessary to secure a really outstanding bird to win. Most important is the "blaže," or scarlet of the face and forehead. This must be shapely and clean-cut, the feathering being a velvety crimson. It should extend well behind the eyes, and when looked at from the front it should appear to run well down the throat. It must be as square as possible at the corners and free from any black striping. The black round the base of the beak should be as narrow as possible. The black feathering on top of the head must be wide and intense in hue, evenly cut and clean at the edges. The white of the cheeks must be well shaped and distinct. The chestnut of the body should be rich in tone, and there should not be too much white on the breast. There are twelve feathers in the flights, each of which has a white spot which fanciers refer to as "buttons." The yellow band on the wings should be deep in color.

The Siberian race of the Goldfinch (*C. c. major*), is larger in size than the British form (5½ in. or 139.7 mm), but must be entered in a separate class for Continental birds at English bird shows.

Siskin *(Carduelis spinus)*

Description: Crown black; a broad yellow streak behind the eye; chin black; body plumage variegated with gray, green and yellow, lighter on the underparts; wings dusky, with a transverse greenish yellow bar, and a black one above, and another black one across the middle of the tertiaries; tail dusky, the base and edge of the inner webs greenish yellow. The hen is duller throughout and lacks the black on the head. Length: four and one-half inches (114 mm.). Habitat: Europe and western Asia.

This little finch makes an ideal cage bird, even wild-caught specimens quickly become tame and on friendly terms with their owner. Indeed, a Siskin can be enticed on to one's hand with a little maw seed a few days after it has been captured. Its one fault in captivity is that it is so greedy that it overeats, becoming very fat and unhealthy. For this reason it should be given very little hemp and maw seed. A better mixture should consist of canary, summer rape and teazle. Seeding wild plants of all kinds can be offered, as well as a little soft-bill mixture and a meal worm now and then. The Siskin is very fond of bathing and should be allowed to do so regularly.

The Siskin is not much of songster, the theme consisting of a few rapid notes terminating in a long, drawn-out cry. It breeds freely in captivity and will hybridize with the canary.

For exhibition purposes a large specimen is needed. Most Siskins are not much more than four and one-half inches in length, so that an outsize one will always gain points on this feature alone. The dark cap must be of good shape and richly laced, and a Siskin possessing a really well-defined bib will always be regarded favorably by the judges.

Hooded Siskin *(C. cucullata)*

Description: Whole head black; upper parts vermilion, brighter on lower back; wings red and black; sides of the neck and underparts vermilion, white on the abdomen. The hen is grayish where the cock is black; her back is slightly washed with vermilion, and the lower back and above the tail are bright vermilion. The wings are orange and gray; the sides of the throat and face ashy gray; breast orange-red. Length: about four and three-fourth inches (118 mm). Habitat: Venezuela and Trinidad. Introduced into Cuba and Puerto Rico.

This lovely little bird, generally called the "Red Siskin," was first brought to England in 1906, when Captain Pam and other collectors for the London Zoological Society brought home a few specimens. Since that time it has been regularly imported, but the price is always very high. When they first arrive, these siskins are very delicate indeed and must be carefully acclimatized to withstand the temperatures of English and United States bird-rooms. For the first week they should be put in a cage placed near a heater, so that the temperature can be kept around eighty degrees Fahrenheit day and night for at least a week. Then you can gradually reduce this temperature, provided the birds seem lively,

Napoleon Weaver. This West African weaver closely resembles the Orange Weaver, although it is easier to breed depending on space and food provided. It will fare better in a roomy aviary than in a cage, and once acclimatized can even winter in an outside flight as long as there is enough protection from North and East and a covered shelter is available.

Rufous-necked Weaver. In the wild these birds are colony breeders and build their nests with numerous other weaver species. In captivity, however, they must be kept in a separate aviary.

Parson Finch. This small Australian bird measures only 4½ inches in length. Although it is one of the best breeders, the sexes are rather difficult to determine.

Cherry Finch. This delicate little bird has never been very popular as an aviary subject due to its frail constitution. It is rather difficult to acclimatize, and fanciers would be well advised to purchase a pair that has been aviary bred. Although it is not as brightly colored as the other Australian seedeaters, the Cherry Finch is still quite an attractive bird.

The Black-headed Siskin is a rather delicate bird, not easily bred in captivity.

until it stands at about sixty-five degrees Fahrenheit. This is the only safe way to establish Red Siskins. Once they have got over the troubles of acclimatization, these birds are no trouble at all, and will live to a good age in captivity.

In disposition the Hooded Siskin is a charming and confiding little bird which will breed readily in either a cage or aviary. It is used for hybridizing with the canary, producing an attractive copper-colored hybrid. Feeding should be on the same lines as advised for the common Siskin except that some millet seed may be added to its mixture. It will also eat cracked sunflower and soaked teazle. When teazle is offered in this way it should be soaked in boiling water for about ten minutes, and then dried by rubbing the seeds in a clean cloth.

Black-headed Siskin *(C. icterica)*

Description: Whole of the head black; olive green above, yellow on the rump; yellow below; tail yellow at the base, black at the tip; wings black, with a broad yellow belt across the base of the flights. The hen is duller, without the black head. Length: about five inches (127 mm). Habitat: Brazil, Argentina, Chile.

At liberty this bird frequents farm land and cultivated places, where flocks may be seen feeding on weeds, especially sow thistle and other composites. It has a very sweet song, much superior to that of the common Siskin of Europe. It is not often offered for sale in England, but is more frequently on the United States markets. The few English aviculturists who have had specimens found them very delicate birds, which did not long survive. It has been exhibited at the London Zoo.

Green Singing Finch *(Serinus mozambicus)*

Description: Top of the head, neck, back, wings and tail greenish gray; throat, eyebrow streak, breast and underparts bright lemon yellow. Hen similar, but less bright in color, and the yellow margins of the wing coverts less distinct. Length: about five inches (127 mm). Habitat: widely distributed over Africa.

This delightful little finch is really more yellow than green, and reminds one of a small Siskin, being rather more slightly built and very active in movements. The sexes are rather alike, though it is not really difficult to select a pair when comparing adult birds, the cock usually being of a brighter yellow while the female has a necklace of black spots across the throat. But this distinction only holds good in birds of the same age, as an old hen would be just as brightly colored as a young cock. The cock, of course, betrays his sex by singing, but he is not in song all the year through, so that unless one has had the bird under observation some months this may not be heard. The song is clear and sweet, and loud for such a small bird.

Green Singing Finches pair only for the breeding season, and then separate. The courtship is inclined to be rough, and usually results in the hen getting some of her feathers pulled out by her intended mate. The courtship lasts about a week, and then the pair settle down. The nest is cup-shaped and an open-type of nest box

Above & Opposite: The Orange Weaver and the Crimson-crowned Weaver are closely related birds. They may be kept together and cared for in the same manner as most other Weavers. Both will tend to become aggressive during the breeding period. Above is pictured an Orange Weaver. Opposite, the two uppermost birds are Crimson-crowned Weavers and the other three are Orange Weavers.

The Green Singing Finch makes a good aviary bird but is
not bred successfully in confined quarters.

is the best to use, or a suitable site can be made with bunches of
brushwood on a shelf in a corner of the aviary. The eggs are pale
blue. The hen incubates, leaving her eggs only for a few minutes
daily. The cock feeds her while she is sitting. The Green Singing
Finch is not often bred successfully, however. Should any young
be hatched, plenty of live food should be provided, as well as soft
food as for canaries.

Hybrids have been produced between the cock singing finch and
the hen canary. For this purpose, select a rather small Border or
Roller hen to ensure fertile eggs, the finch being such a small bird.

The Green Singing Finch makes a good aviary bird and is perfectly hardy when acclimatized. No heat is required in an outdoor aviary, provided it has a dry, draft-proof, well-lighted shelter in which the birds can retire at night. Though normally good mixers with other small finches, cocks in breeding condition have been known to become spiteful, so it is better not to associate mated pairs with small waxbills, except in a spacious aviary.

Gray Singing Finch (*S. leucopygius*)

Description: Upper parts ashy brown, the centers of the feathers being darker, the crown being more distinct gray than the back; rump white; wings and tail dark brown, with paler edges to the feathers; throat white; breast gray, mottled with ashy brown. Length: about four and one half inches (114.3 mm). Habitat: northeastern and Equatorial Africa.

Though not so pretty as the last species, the Gray Singing Finch is a great favorite with fanciers. It is lively and energetic, of amiable disposition and a fine songster. The strength of its voice and the energy with which the song is poured out is quite astonishing, and the little bird will sit on a branch and sing away almost incessantly hour after hour. It is very hardy, and an ideal bird for the outdoor aviary among such companions as waxbills, mannikins and the like. The sexes are similar, but the free-singing cocks are easily picked out from the silent hens.

While quite harmless with even the smallest birds of other species, they sometimes quarrel among themselves, but most of it is of a playful nature, and the birds which a moment before were engaged in what looked like a desperate encounter will be found seated or feeding together and the best of friends.

The Gray Singing Finch breeds more readily than the Green species, preferring an ordinary canary nest pan in which to build. It will hybridize with the canary, and though the results of such a cross are not striking in appearance, they are nice pets and excellent songsters.

Singing finches and other Serins should be fed on a staple diet made up of two parts canary, one part white millet, one-half part Indian millet, one-half part summer rape, one-fourth part teazle with a little maw seed added now and then. They are also fond of

Green Singing Finch. A close relative of the canary, this bird has a delightful song and will sing almost constantly. It can be kept with small finches in a cage or aviary. They will breed more readily in a cage or indoor aviary where a reasonably warm temperature can be maintained.

Indian Spice or Nutmeg Finch. This is one of the best known species of all finches and is always available. It is difficult to obtain a true pair, but should a pair begin to nest, they must be given absolute quiet. Any slight disturbance could seriously hamper any breeding attempts, and any success is doubtful.

St. Helena Waxbill. These delicate birds cannot stand cold, damp weather and must spend the winter in a warm room. They will nest readily and one pair can be kept in an indoor aviary with other small (4-4½″) birds.

Dufresne's Waxbill. Although this bird has been rarely imported, it has been bred successfully in Europe. It is best suited for an indoor aviary.

soaked teazle, spray millet (*Panicum*), green food of various kinds, seeding grasses, and occasionally fruit and insects.

A number of other Serins have been imported, among which may be mentioned the Cape Canary (*S. canicollis*), a thick-set yellow bird, greenish on the upper parts. It has a song which has been likened to that of a Roller Canary, and is a popular cage bird in South Africa. It has bred and hybridized in England, but is considered very difficult to breed.

The Sulphur Seed-eater (*S. sulphuratus*) is another heavily-built bird from southern Africa, with a big beak. It is, however, quite a safe companion for other small birds. It is greenish yellow streaked with blackish above, except on the rump; wings blackish with yellow edges; below yellowish; a broad golden yellow eyebrow streak. The hen is smaller and duller.

The Himalayan Seed-eater or Red-fronted Siskin *(S. pusillus)* is an attractive bird, and a nice singer, but rare in captivity. It is easily distinguished by its vermilion red forehead and crown. The breast and sides of the body are yellow, marked with black. The upper parts are brown, with yellow edges to the feathers. It is a native of the Caucasus and North Persia to Turkistan, wintering in Asia Minor, Lebanon and the northwestern Himalayas. It is the only serin that naturally has red in its plumage.

Alario Finch *(Serinus alario)*

Description: Head all around, throat and stripe on each side of the breast, black; a white collar passing around the sides and back of the neck; upper parts cinnamon red; remainder of underparts white. The hen is paler and more gray, the chestnut of the cock being replaced by coffee color; throat and breast gray, mottled with black; below white, washed with buff on the flanks. Length: five and one-half inches (140 mm). Habitat: South Africa.

This is a handsome finch, active and engaging in habits, and one which quickly becomes adapted to cage life. It has a soft pleasing little flute-like song, but is said to be very imitative, and when associated with canaries or Linnets it quickly substitutes their songs for its own. It hybridizes readily with the canary, producing a handsome cross, and quite the finest hybrid songster one could wish to hear. It is hardy and can safely be wintered in an outdoor aviary. Unfortunately it is seldom imported nowadays, owing to the tightening some years ago of the bird protection laws in South Africa.

Common Rosefinch *(Carpodacus erythrina)*

Description: Dull crimson, mixed with brownish above; color brightest on rump, throat and breast, fading to white under the tail; wings and tail brown-edged with rufous. In breeding plumage, the margins wear off the feathers and so leave the bird a brighter crimson. The hen is olive-brown, streaked with brown; wings and tail margined with ochraceous; a double white bar across the wing coverts; beak horny brown; legs dusky; eyes dark brown. Length: six inches (152.4 mm). Habitat: widely distributed over eastern Europe and Asia.

Unfortunately, the lovely rosy hue of these birds is apt to fade in captivity and is replaced by dull yellow. It is fairly frequently imported, and is confiding and gentle in captivity, requiring the same treatment as for a Linnet. At liberty the birds are said to be met with in flocks during winter migration, when they feed on millet crops, wild cherries, mulberries and a variety of other seeds and fruits. Buds and shoots are also eaten. It also partakes of the nectar of the flowering tree, *Erythrina*. The cock has a pleasant but somewhat monotonous song. The nest is cup-shaped, placed in low bushes, and the clutch consists of three or four eggs. They are of a beautiful deep blue, with a few scrawls and spots of brown or blackish.

Linnet *(Acanthis cannabina)*

Description: Head brown, feathers dusky in the centers, those of the forehead more or less tinged with crimson; upper parts chestnut. Tail blackish, edged white; breast dull crimson, or brown; abdomen dull white; beak brownish horn color, more bluish in summer. Length: five and a half inches (139.7 mm). Habitat: Europe and Western Asia.

The Linnet is one of the most popular of British finches, being hardy, easily maintained, a good breeder in captivity, and having a very sweet and varied song. The sexes can be distinguished at all seasons by comparing the white outer borders of the primaries; these are much wider in the cock than in the hen. The Linnet varies seasonally in its plumage, and unfortunately cock Linnets in

Bullfinch. The song of the Bullfinch is almost inaudible, but they have the remarkable ability to perfectly imitate the calls of other birds. They can even be taught to imitate the tunes of popular songs and, once learned, they are never forgotten.

captivity do not get the beautiful carmine shading on the head and breast so characterisitc of the wild birds, especially in spring.

As an aviary bird, the Linnet is gentle and not in the least offensive towards other birds. It should be kept on a rather plain diet and given plenty of room to exercise through the winter to get the birds into good breeding condition.

For exhibition purposes a Linnet must be large, with the markings clear and well-defined throughout, with well-laced thighs. The wings and tail must be close and compact, with well-defined white feathers, and the general color must be rich nut brown.

The Twite (*A. flavirostris*), which is found in the mountainous parts of Britain as well as in Norway, Lapland, Turkey and Asia, is only worth keeping if one is specializing in British finches. It is a streaky brown bird with a yellow bill and a little white on the wings, and is of the same size as a Linnet. The cock has some pink above the tail, which is permanent in captivity. Dr. Butler says he found it "greedy, selfish and quarrelsome". It has been bred in captivity.

Mealy Redpoll *(A. f. flammea)*

Description: Forehead, throat and lores black; crown deep crimson; below light crimson tinged with buff, fading towards the tail into white; upper parts nut brown with dusky streaks; wings and tail dusky, edged with pale reddish brown. The hen is much duller throughout. Length: five and one half inches (139.7 mm). Habitat: northern Europe (from Scandinavia eastward through European Russia).

This is a cheerful little finch, very hardy, lively and intelligent. In an aviary, however, it is inclined to be mischievous and may pull other birds' nests to pieces. Unfortunately, after a molt in captivity, the Redpoll loses the beautiful crimson on the crown, which becomes a glossy bronze hue. In size it about equals a Siskin, and is equally intelligent, acquiring many engaging tricks and habits. A pet Redpoll usually becomes so tame that it can be allowed a certain amount of liberty, as it will return to its cage. The song is rather ample, twittering and pleasant.

Redpolls nest freely in aviaries, and have been bred in cages about three feet by two feet by eighteen inches. They are in general inoffensive birds and can be housed together or along with other pairs of finches. The natural nesting period is from May onward, and they often build several nests before finally selecting a site that suits them. When the eggs are laid the hen sits closely, and the cock feeds her assiduously. The eggs hatch in a fortnight, when live and soft food should be offered. The young birds leave the nest at twelve to fourteen days, but often return to sit in the nest again. Nesting material should consist of hay, grasses, cotton-wool, strips of bark, and cut lengths of coarse string. Both parents are usually good feeders, and the nestlings are the best of all our finches at weaning themselves from their parents and becoming self-supporting.

An ideal exhibition Redpoll must be as large as possible, with a good head, neck, and chest. The color should be a rich brown, with profuse and distinct dark stripes down the flanks, and if these extend across the breast all the better. The cap should be deep and rich in color and red for preference. A neat black bib of good size should cover the area immediately below the bird's beak. The bars on the wings should show distinctly. Hens are said to make the best exhibition birds since a well-marked one of this sex will retain her colors, whereas a good cock will lose his best markings after a couple of molts.

The Lesser Redpoll (*A.f. cabaret*) is a smaller and generally browner-colored subspecies occurring in Britain. It is the most frequently offered for sale.

Greenfinch (*Chloris chloris*) (recently changed in *Carduelis chloris*)

Description: Yellowish green, variegated with yellow and dusky. Length: six inches (152.4 mm). Habitat: Europe.

The Greenfinch is a particularly hardy bird, but is a poor singer, and inclined to be greedy and spiteful in an aviary with smaller birds. It will do well on canary and rape as a staple food, with sunflower added daily, and plenty of wild seeds and green food. In winter some hemp, linseed and teazle can be offered. It is a good exhibition bird, and fanciers will find that regular spraying of the plumage with soft water improves the natural color and helps to give the bird that soft, silky plumage which is so much admired.

A good exhibition Greenfinch should be fairly large, with a good bold head, not pinched over the beak, or narrow at the back. It

Greenfinches are hardy birds which are very easily bred. They are rather poor singers, however.

should have a nice thick neck and broad chest in proportion, and its color should be one even tone all over the body. Some fanciers prefer to see color-fed Greenfinches, but others declare the natural shade to be all that is desired.

Greenfinches will breed freely in an aviary. The sexes are not difficult to distinguish, the hen lacking the brightness of plumage of her mate. This is especially noticeable in the wing bars. She is also rather smaller. Young Greenfinches are very subject to diarrhea after they have left the nest, and losses from this cause are frequent, although the mortality may be reduced dramatically if large doses of total vitamin complex and mineral trace elements are given.

Crossbill *(Loxia curvirostra)*

Description: The plumage is very variable, according to age and sex. It is a mixture of green, orange, yellow, and brick red. Length: six and one-half inches (164 mm). Habitat: northern Africa, northern Europe and Asia (Ireland to Japan), and North America (from Alaska to Newfoundland, southward to Mexico).

This is one of the most interesting of British birds. With its curiously twisted beak, the Crossbill is able to attack pine cones, inserting the partly opened beak below the scales and wrenching them off with a swift sideways movement of the head. It sometimes enters orchards and bores holes in apples to eat the pips. It can open almond nuts in the same way, but is equally adept at shelling small seeds.

In disposition the Crossbill is very tame, and it is hardy in the extreme, but is sometimes destructive to the woodwork of its cage or aviary, where it climbs about like a parrot. It has bred in captivity, but this is not a common event. Crossbills will eat any seed mixture, and an ideal one would consist of three parts sunflower, one part buckwheat, one part canary and some oats. Fir cones should be given when it is possible to obtain these. It is gentle with other birds in an aviary.

Bullfinch *(Pyrrhula pyrrhula)*

Description: Crown, throat, around the beak, wings and tail jet black; underparts rich red; back gray; rump and abdomen white; a broad buff and gray band across the wings. The hen has the rich red of the lower parts replaced by reddish brown. Beak black. Length: up to seven and one half inches (190.5 mm). Habitat: Europe. There are some ten subspecies.

The Bullfinch is one of the handsomest of British birds, and makes a charming cage pet or inhabitant of a garden aviary. The cock has a gray back and red breast, while in the hen the back is drab and the breast is chocolate. As a wild bird it is generally seen in pairs, and favors woodland districts.

In disposition the Bullfinch is amiable, and can be trusted in an aviary even with weaker species. In such an accommodation it will

The Bullfinch is an attractive, amiable bird which can be taught to sing up to two short tunes. Shown is a male Bullfinch.

readily breed, though it seldom does so in a cage. The cock Bullfinch is no use for hybridization but the hen will mate with almost any other typical finch, including the canary.

Aviary-bred Bullfinches make charming pets, and they can be taught to pipe a tune. Hens learn to pipe as well as cocks. Its natural note is a plaintive cry.

The usual method of teaching a Bullfinch to pipe is to hand-rear young birds taken from the nest when about nine days old. The birds are caged separately when about a month old, and tunes are whistled or played to them in slow time fifteen to twenty times a day. This tuition is carried on for at least nine months. Individual birds vary in their ability to learn to pipe. Tunes of about six lines are about as much as the birds can pick up, but they can frequently be taught two short tunes. Tunes in the keys of F, G and A major suit them best. Sometimes a bird only learns a line or two of

Female Bullfinch. Female Bullfinches are often used in crossbreeding experiments.

the tune, and these are called "broken pipers." Well-trained birds will pipe when told to do so by their owner.

A more generous diet is necessary for the Bullfinch than for other finches, as it feeds on buds, fruit, insects, small snails, grubs and the like, as well as grass seeds, dandelions, thistles and knapweed, etc. In spring sprigs containing bursting buds of such trees as beech, birch, hawthorn, and oak, and any kind of fruit tree prunings should be given. In summer and autumn berried fruits are an important item in the Bullie's diet. It especially favors blackberries, elderberries, hips, haws, and privet berries. Yew berries are dangerous and should not be offered to any birds. The "keys" of the ash tree are much appreciated by Bullfinches, as also are the seed-heads of dock, persicaria, sow thistle, shepherd's purse, meadow grass and chickweed. Of ordinary bird seeds, give a mixture of canary, summer rape, winter rape, teazle, and a few sunflower seeds daily.

The Bullfinch is an excellent exhibition bird, and a likely winner should be shapely, thick-set, short and cobby, with a well-fitted breast, a broad skull, and neck and throat full and short. The shoulders should be broad but not prominent, the back well filled in, the wings tight against the body, and the carriage graceful. Colors are important. The bill must be black and shiny, and the cap clean-cut, of a velvety hue. The back should be silver gray, even in color, and free from smokiness. The breast color must be rich and bright, and run even in tone down to the thighs.

The Siberian Bullfinch is similar to the British bird, but very much larger.

Pine Grosbeak *(Pinicola enucleator)*

Description: Head and upper parts of the neck reddish orange, steaked on the back with gray; wings and tail black, the former with two white bars, the primaries and tail feathers edged with orange, the secondaries with white; underparts dull vinous, the feathers gray at the base, and with dusky V-shaped subterminal markings. The hen is coppery bronze, slightly olivaceous on the back and more golden on the rump. Length: eight inches (203.2 mm). Habitat: Arctic regions during summer, coming southwards in Europe and North America in winter.

This fine bird is seldom seen in captivity. Unfortunately, after a molt in cage or aviary, the lovely wine-rose hue is replaced by dull yellowish.

The Pine Grosbeak, like most Arctic birds, is quite fearless of humans, and makes a very confiding pet. It has been bred in captivity by Mr. St. Quentin. The food consists of seeds of conifers, and in captivity it should be supplied with sunflower seeds, berries, buds, insects, and earthworms. Dr. Butler says the berries of the Rowan (mountain ash) are very poisonous to these birds. Yet they form one of its chief foods in the wild state.

This bird is also found in the United States, where it is hailed with enthusiasm on account of its lovely color. The note is a loud, clear whistle, uttered when the bird is on the wing. In spring it has a melodious song.

V Buntings

The Buntings (*Emberizinae*) contain some of the most beautiful of all cage and aviary birds in the American species. The true buntings, however, are rather somberly clad birds. Their nests are cup-shaped and placed on the ground among herbage, or in low, thick bushes, and the usual number of eggs is from four to six. They are decidedly more insectivorous than the other finches, and when breeding in aviaries insects are a necessity, and soft food should always be available. Seed mixtures should contain canary, millet, oats and hemp, grass and grass seeds. Soft food should be an insectile mixture, with which is incorporated grated carrot and chopped chickweed. They much appreciate soaked oats or wheat, or summer rape which is just commencing to sprout.

The Reed Bunting is a handsome, non-aggressive bird.

Reed Bunting *(Emberiza schoeniclus)*

Description: Head, throat, and gorget are black (speckled with brown in winter); nape, sides of the neck, and a line extending to the base of the beak on each side, white; chestnut and dusky above; below white, streaked with dusky on the flanks. The hen has a reddish brown head, with dusky spots; the white on the neck less distinct; below reddish white with dusky spots. Length: six to seven inches (152.4-177.8 mm). Habitat: Europe.

The Reed Bunting is a common, resident species in Britain, frequenting marshy places and watersides, and spending much of its time hiding in reed beds. Its natural food consists largely of the seeds of rushes together with insects. The cock is quite a handsome bird in his spring plumage with a black head and bib, white collar and a reddish brown back. The tail is black with white patches on the outside feathers.

As an aviary bird, the Reed Bunting is by no means aggressive, but is shy and retiring by nature, though not actually nervous of one's presence. Its song consists of three or four short notes and then two or three sharp ones to terminate it.

Golden-breasted Bunting *(E. flaviventris)*

Description: Chestnut-red above, rump and upper tail coverts ash gray; wings gray with black and white markings; flights black edged with white excepting the inner secondaries which are edged with chestnut; tail black, edged with gray, the four outermost tipped with white; head black, with white streaks; yellow below, orange on the chest, gray on the thighs; upper mandible black, lower mandible brown. The hen has the chestnut of the upper parts deeper and streaked with black. Length: six and one-half inches (165.1 mm). Habitat: South Africa, northward to Angola and Eritrea.

This is one of the prettiest of the typical buntings, and the cock utters a very sweet, soft little song. It becomes remarkably tame in an aviary, and is harmless to other birds. It spends much of its time on the ground, and besides the usual seed mixture, insects should be given. Like most buntings, the Golden-breasted is not really suited to cage life, as it is apt to become too fat under such restricted conditions.

At liberty the bird breeds during midsummer, constructing a cupshaped nest of fine grasses and fibrous material in a bush, usually only a few feet from the ground. The eggs are glossy white, with purplish olive and dark brown markings at the large end. After the breeding season the birds gather in small flocks.

Black-headed Bunting *(E. melanocephala)*

Description: The cock in full breeding plumage is a handsome and distinctive bird. The crown and cheeks are jet black, the tail mostly brown and the underparts clear yellow. In winter the head becomes more brownish, and both chestnut and yellow are less rich owing to the buff tips of the feathers. The hen resembles the cock, but never acquires such an intensely black head, this being brownish with just a touch of black. Below she is more buff than yellow, though in summer this is rather richer in tone. Length: seven and one-half inches (190.5 mm). Habitat: south Europe, eastwards to northwest and central India. A few have been taken in Britain.

The Black-headed Bunting is a migratory bird, and mostly seen in flocks, often of vast size. They feed in the ripening crops, and when flushed fly off to the nearest tree, making it appear a mass of yellow. The birds breed in western Asia and southeastern Europe. The nest is cupshaped, of grasses lined with hair and roots, and is usually placed in a bush, vine, or small tree. Four to six eggs are laid, and these are pale greenish blue, spotted with ashy brown and gray.

This abundant, attractive, and widely distributed bird is not often seen in captivity, in Europe at any rate.

Cirl Bunting *(E. cirlus)*

Description: Crown dark olive streaked with black; gorget and band above and below the eye yellow; chin and throat, and a band across the eye black; below the black of the throat a bright yellow band, then one of sage green; back light brown, with dusky marks; chest warm chestnut color; outside tail feathers white. In the hen the distinct patches of black and yellow are wanting; dusky spots on the back larger. Length: six and one half inches (165.1 mm). Habitat: Europe.

With the exception of its black throat, this bird resembles the Yellow-hammer, and its habits are also very similar. It is a quietly pretty bird, and a favorite bunting among British bird fanciers.

It is a local bird in Britain, and mostly to be seen on the southern slopes of the South Downs, where its shrill and penetrating note may be frequently heard. The song resembles that of the Yellow-hammer, except for the absence of the terminal double note. It is not aggressive as an aviary bird, and is easily kept on various kinds of cereals, mixed seeds, wild grass seeds and live food. The Cirl Bunting makes a splendid show bird, and for this purpose the olive green of the crown should show distinct streaks, the yellow stripes above and below the eye must be clear, brilliant and free from blemish. The back of the throat should form a bib with bands extending to the sides of the neck, and be bordered by a lemon yellow collar.

Yellow Bunting *(E. citrinella)*

Description: Head, neck, breast and underparts bright yellow, more or less streaked with dusky; flanks streaked with chestnut; reddish brown above, spotted with darker. The hen has the yellow parts less vivid, and spotted with dull reddish brown. Length six and one-half to eight inches (165-203 mm). Habitat: Europe.

The Yellow-hammer, as this bird is generally called, is one of the commonest wild birds in Britain, and the best known of the buntings as a cage and aviary bird. It is easily maintained on canary seed, oats, and a few meal worms. A mixed seed may also be offered, but little of this will be taken while canary seed is available. Twice a week a spoonful of insectile food, prepared as for soft-bills, should be given, as well as the usual green food in season.

The Yellow-hammer is not often bred in captivity, and show specimens are usually wild-caught birds, young ones taken in the autumn being best for the purpose. Some of these will only show a portion of their adult plumage around the head and neck. This should be bright in color.

For exhibition purposes, a large, well-marked bird is required. The yellow of the head should be as rich as possible, and a clear, dark line should run from the back of the skull on each side of the head meeting in V-shaped form just above the base of the upper

The Yellow Bunting is quite a common bird in much of Europe.

mandible. There should be regular and distinct spangling on the back. Color in Yellow-hammers improves with age.

Other members of the genus *Emberiza* are occasionally seen at bird shows. The Ortolan *(E. hortulana)* which was once commonly imported to Britain, has been rare as a cage bird for many years. The Little Bunting (*E. pusilla*) is a rather sparrow-like bird with a white line from above the eye to the side of the neck, but smaller than a Reed Bunting. It is a native of Finland, due east to Siberia and Turkistan. A few reach Scotland in winter. The Red-headed Bunting *(E. bruniceps)* actually has a crown of golden sienna hue with specks of dusky gray. It has an olive-streaked back, yellow rump, brown wings and tail, chestnut about the head and breast, and rich yellow below. It comes from Siberia, central Asia, and India. This species has been frequently imported into Britain, and has often been bred in captivity since 1973. The Corn Bunting (*E. miliaris*) has little to recommend it as a cage or aviary bird, being large in size, dull brownish in plumage and having a harsh, unmelodious song.

Snow Bunting *(Plectrophenax nivalis)*

Description: The cock in full breeding plumage is very striking, being white, with the back, flights and middle tail feathers black; beak black in summer, yellow in winter; after the autumn molt the feathers of the upper parts, breast and flanks become bordered with dull chestnut. All the black parts of the hen's plumage are grayer, with pale edges to the feathers; head and neck mottled with blackish. Length: six and one-half inches (165.1 mm). Habitat: Arctic regions.

The Snow Bunting is a winter visitor to the north of Britain, and a few pairs remain to breed in the Highlands of Scotland (above 3,000 ft.). The birds also migrate as far south as the northern half of the United States in cold weather, where their appearance is a sure sign that winter has begun in earnest. Large flocks may sometimes be seen flying rather low along the shore, or over cultivated fields, moving in an undulating line, uttering soft, low calls resembling those of a Linnet, but intermixed at times with a sort of stifled scream or churr. On the ground, this attractive bunting is very lark-like, running quickly and not hopping like most finches. In its brown winter plumage it also resembles a lark in color, as it does also in size.

Lapland Bunting *(Calcarius lapponicus)*

Description: The cock in breeding plumage, which is not assumed until the bird is two years old, has a velvety black head, neck and throat, with a white line from the base of the upper mandible passing over the eye to the sides of the neck; a broad chestnut belt across the nape; rest of upper plumage and wings a pleasing combination of rich black and brown on a whitish ground; below white, with black streaks on the flanks. The hen is paler, without the chestnut collar, and has a whitish stripe down the center of the head and a black line below the cheeks to the upper throat; the dark feathers of the crown have chestnut borders. Length: five and one-half—six and one-half inches (139.7-165.1 mm). Habitat: the

Lapland Bunting inhabits much of the circumpolar regions, breeding at high altitudes in Norway, but in any suitable locality in Lapland and north Siberia. It migrates southward, and small numbers reach the British Isles, but unlike the Snow Bunting, it is not known to breed there.

This fine bunting is largely a ground bird, with the hind claw long and nearly straight, as in larks and pipits. It is an excellent aviary bird, being inoffensive, attractive in coloring, and having quite a melodious song, combining that of the Skylark and the Linnet. At liberty, it sings while soaring, and the hen has a song nearly equal to that of the cock.

After the molt the cock wears a winter dress, in which he is soberly colored like the hen. This is unfortunate from an exhibitor's point of view, as shows take place in winter, so that it is difficult to bench this bird at its best.

America is very rich in buntings, some of which are fine songsters, like the White-shouldered Lark Bunting, *Calamospiza melanocorys*, which the London Zoo first acquired in 1901. There are also numerous song sparrows (*Zonotrichia*) and a number of others which are hardly ever seen outside their native country as cage birds.

Nonpareil Bunting *(Passerina ciris)*

Description: Crown, cheeks and shoulders rich blue; back golden green, becoming orange on the rump and yellow at the base of the tail; wings and tail bronze-green; whole of the underparts bright scarlet. The hen is almost as pretty, but has green instead of bright blue about the head and mantle. Length: about five and one-half inches (139.7 mm). Habitat: southern United States of America, Cuba, Bahamas, and Central America to Panama.

At liberty this magnificent bunting haunts the thickets of the forests, where the cock may be heard singing from a tall shrub or other commanding position. The nest is placed in low bushes, and the hen sits so close that she will sometimes allow herself to be picked up in the hand rather than leave her nest. The eggs are white with purplish-brown spots.

In an aviary this is a most attractive bird, but unfortunately the scarlet of the cock is apt to change slowly to yellowish. This is less

The Nonpareil (or Painted) Bunting is a colorful bird which makes a fine pet.

likely to happen if the bird is kept in a large sunny aviary and given plenty of insect food. It is comparatively hardy when acclimatized, but is not a safe companion for closely related species, being rather pugnacious toward them. It makes a fine pet, becoming very tame and learning to take tidbits from the fingers. It has been bred in captivity, but this is not a common occurrence, perhaps because hens are not often obtainable on the (English) market.

Rainbow Bunting *(P. leclancheri)*

Description: General color above cobalt blue, washed with dull green on the mantle and upper back; wing coverts, blue; tail, pale greenish blue; crown, yellowish green with the sides of the head and nape blue; underside, rich golden yellow, becoming orange-red on the breast. The hen is much duller than the cock, being olive green above, brighter on the rump, and with a blue tail. Below, she is yellow. Length: about five inches (127 mm). Habitat: western Mexico.

This is one of the most attractive of foreign cage birds, and the first specimens arrived in England in 1909. Three years later the London Zoo received a few, but it did not arrive in any numbers on the bird market until the 1930's, when Messrs. Chapman brought over big consignments. When newly arrived the species suffers from the effect of damp climate, and it is not hardy out-of-doors during the winter months. But it is not unduly delicate, and requires no heat when kept indoors. The main thing is to insure that the winter quarters are proof against drafts and damp.

Rainbow Buntings are excellent cage birds, but being active they should have ample quarters, and a cage for a pair should not be less than two feet long. In disposition they are good-tempered, and agree with other small seed eaters, and would breed in a naturally planted aviary. The cocks sing quite pleasantly.

Rainbow and allied buntings should be fed on a varied diet consisting of a seed mixture made up of two parts canary, one part millet, and a little Indian millet and groats added. Offer in addition some good quality soft-bill mixture, fruit of various kinds, seeding grasses and weeds, two or three meal worms or other insects daily, a millet spray, and live ant's eggs or gentles when available.

Exhibition specimens of this and the Nonpareil Bunting are usually color-fed, with the color food prepared and sold for color-feeding canaries. This is because they tend to lose their rich tones after a molt or two in confinement, particularly when caged.

Lazuli Bunting *(P. amoena)*

Description: Turquoise blue above, more greenish in the middle of the back; wings and tail blackish, edged with blue; the white

112

ends of the wing coverts form two bands across the wings; lores, black; sides of the head, throat, and sides of breast, bright blue; the upper breast brownish chestnut, separated from the blue throat by an ill-defined white crescent; the remainder of the underparts white; beak black, bluish below; feet black; eyes brown. The hen is dull brown above; wings and tail dusky, with greenish blue edgings; buff bands across the wing; below buff, deeper on the chest, fading to white under the tail. Immature birds are grayish brown above, white below with a buff tinge, and some streaks on the breast. Length: five and one-half inches (139 mm). Habitat: breeds from southern British Columbia, southern Alberta, southeastern Saskatchewan, Montana and western North Dakota south to western Texas, northern New Mexico, Arizona and southern California. It winters in Mexico.

This beautiful bird is strictly protected, and in consequence very few examples find their way to English bird-rooms and aviaries. Those exported come from Mexico, where bird laws are not so stringent as in the United States. In captivity it does well and requires the same treatment as others of the genus. Canary and millet seed should be given, and insect fare, as small meal worms and larvae, etc. In Britain and similar climates it is best kept indoors in the winter, though it does not require artificial heat in normal seasons. The cock has a cheerful little song, but the normal call is a sharp sound like "Quit!"

It breeds in the vicinity of water as a rule, attaching its nest to reed stalks or bushes. The nest is made of grass blades firmly interwoven, and is lined with horsehair and cobwebs.

Indigo Bunting (*Passerina cyanea*)

Description: Head and throat, deep purplish blue, becoming lighter on the back and above the tail; wings and tail a brownish black, edged with blue. Winter plumage, brownish like the hen, mottled with blue. The hen is brown above, darker on the wings and tail; breast grayish, washed and faintly streaked with brown, lighter on the abdomen. Length: six inches (152.4 mm). Habitat: eastern North America, wintering from southern Mexico to Panama.

The Indigo Bunting is a most desirable bird for cage or aviary, and it has crossed with the canary, producing green hybrids. It was first bred by Mr. Farrar in 1900. The song is a burst of melody, somewhat like that of a canary, loud, clear and sweet.

Pileated Finch *(Coryphospingus pileatus)*

Description: Dark, slate gray above, paler toward the tail, which is black; crown black, with a broad central band of shining carmine feathers, which can be raised into a crest; sides of the head, throat, breast and flanks gray; rest of the underparts white. Length: five and one-half inches (139 mm). Habitat: Brazil to Venezuela and Colombia.

Though not a songster, this is a particularly charming little finch, and it is very common on the market. It is harmless in a mixed collection, and was first bred in an aviary by Mrs. Howard Williams in 1905, the birds building an open nest in a laurel bush. Two young ones were reared, and an account was duly published in the *Avicultural Magazine*, n.s. Vol. IV, pp. 30-40.

The Red-crested Finch (*C. cristatus*) is a similar bird, but the body plumage is almost entirely red, the crest being a particularly brilliant vermilion, edged with black. It inhabits Ecuador, Peru, Bolivia, Brazil, Argentina, and Paraguay, but is not imported very often. It is a delightful aviary bird, very peaceful in disposition, and has a way of hopping about shuffling its wings and raising its pretty crest whenever at all excited. Both these birds should be treated as advised for the buntings, and they must have a certain amount of insect fare.

The Black-crested Finch *(Lophospingus pusillus)* is mainly black, white and gray, with a black crest, slightly recurved at the tip. It is about five inches in length. The hen is slaty gray where the cock is an intense black. It will breed fairly freely in an aviary, but live food must be supplied as the young birds are fed entirely on insect fare. This finch is a native of South America.

Saffron Finch *(Sycalis flaveola)*

Description: Bright greenish yellow above, streaked with dusky lines on the mantle; wing and tail feathers dark, edged with yellow; forehead orange, crown and back of the neck bright greenish yellow; underparts bright yellow; beak brownish gray, lower mandible pale; legs and feet dark flesh color. The hen is duller above and paler beneath. The color seems to intensify with age and old hens are sometimes more vividly hued than young cocks in their first adult plumage. Length: six inches (152.4 mm). Habitat: southern Brazil, Venezuela to New Granada.

Though it is sometimes spiteful and tempestuous with weaker birds, the Brazilian Saffron Finch is a popular aviary bird and is a suitable companion for weavers, Java Sparrows, Cut-throats and other strong species. It is hardy and easy to cater for, canary, millet, oats and plenty of green food being suitable fare. Once acclimatized, Saffron Finches can withstand the English winter without any artificial heat. It nests readily in either cage or aviary, using a covered nest box about six inches square. When breeding, gentles should be given and soft-bill mixture, or bread and milk. Its song is hearty but not particularly melodious.

Pelzeln's Saffron Finch (*S.f. pelzelni*) is less often seen on the market. It comes from Brazil, Paraguay and Argentina. In this species the hen is colored differently from the cock. The cock is yellowish green, streaked with black on the back. The wings and tail are black, edged yellow. The lower back is dull yellow, forehead orange, sides of the head and below bright yellow. Some dark streaks on the flanks. Beak, dark horn; feet, brownish; eyes brown. The hen is dull brownish gray above, mottled with darker. The underparts are dirty white, with dusky streaks on the breast. It does not appear to differ much in habits from the better known species.

VI Cardinals
And Grosbeaks

All the cardinals are American birds and are larger and stronger than most species of finches commonly imported to Britain. They are handsome birds in appearance, but very nervous and wild in disposition. They are inclined to be spiteful, and should not be mixed with canaries or other small birds.

The Virginian Cardinal is probably the least quarrelsome with other species, but in mixed company the Red-crested and Pope Cardinals are at times responsible for losses, and there is always a considerable risk in enclosing them with birds smaller than Cockatiels and medium-sized doves.

Except for the Virginian Cardinal they are not good songsters, so are hardly worth keeping in a cage. But if caged, they will thrive well enough, but such active birds should never be kept permanently in a cage less than three feet in length. The ideal accommodation is to devote a small garden aviary to a single pair. They may breed under such conditions, and should be encouraged to do so by fixing up an old thrush or blackbird's nest in a secluded position, preferably in an evergreen bush.

Live food is essential for cardinals when rearing young, and this should be plentiful and varied. Gentles are a suitable and easily secured live food for these large finches.

A satisfactory seed mixture for cardinals consists of one part each canary and millet, one-fourth part sunflower, one-eighth part hemp and a few oats. In addition give four to six meal worms per bird three times weekly, and once or twice some prepared soft-bill mixture. They are fond of soaked wheat, oats, and barley. Caged specimens are better without any hemp.

Red or Virginian Cardinal *(Cardinalis cardinalis)*
Description: Soft rich red, except for a black throat, a black band encircling the beak, and in winter a grayish tinge to the wings. Beak large, heavy, and light red; red pointed crest, large

The Venezuelan or Purple Cardinal is a hardy, gentle bird.

and conspicuous, which can be raised and lowered at will. The hen is gray-brown above, pale buff below; crest, wings, and tail brick-red; throat and band about bill grayish black. Length: eight -nine inches (203-229 mm). Habitat: ranges from the northeastern states of the United States to northern Mexico. There are races in Central America and a similar species in Venezuela.

The Red Cardinal is a prime favorite in its own country, and the United States Department of Agriculture says that one-fourth of its food consists of insects, and that it has "a record for feeding on many of the worst agricultural pests." Trapping of the bird is not allowed in the United States, and those specimens which reach the English bird market come from Mexico.

It has been known as a cage bird for at least two hundred years, and is still very popular with fanciers, being a bold, smart-looking bird and not too aggressive in spite of its Satanic appearance. It can be quite safely kept in an aviary of medium-sized birds, or larger ones.

The Red Cardinal is perfectly hardy out-of-doors in the English winter, and will go to nest readily in a naturally planted aviary. It will nest in a thick bush, or will use a suitable nest box or shelf on which some brushwood has been placed. A regular supply of gentles, caterpillars, grubs, etc., must be given when they have young to rear. But meal worms must be very sparingly given. These insects are very stimulating, and an overgenerous supply causes the birds to kill or throw their young out of the nest, and start building again. The Red Cardinal cannot stand heat waves at all well.

If kept in a cage, this fine bird will soon become tame, but the plumage is apt to gradually fade with each successive molt. The song of the cock is a loud, clear, yet sweet and mellow whistle *"cheer, cheer, he-u, he-u, he-u,"* repeated rapidly with descending inflection, and with nearly an octave in range. The hen also sings, her voice being a soft, melodious warbling.

Venezuelan or Purple Cardinal *(C. phoeniceus)*

Description: Upper parts rich vermilion, lighter on the rump; scarlet crest, long, upright and slightly curled forward at the tip; a narrow frontal line, lores, a small spot at the base of the cheeks, and the chin black; head and underparts rich scarlet; lesser wing coverts scarlet, greater coverts dusky gray-brown with red edges; tail vermilion, dusky at the tip; beak strongly curved, deeper than it is broad, gray in color. The hen is mostly brownish buff above, paler on the rump; crown and nape ashy; crest dark vermilion with dusky tips; a small, black spot beneath the beak; wings dusky, tinged with vermilion; tail dull vermilion, dusky at tip, with ochreous edges to the feathers; lores and below the eye white; ear coverts gray; underparts buff, grayish on throat and paler on the abdomen. Length: about seven and one-half inches (190.5 mm). Habitat: Venezuela, Trinidad, and Colombia.

This handsome bird is commonly called the Phoenix Cardinal, and is seldom seen as a cage bird in Britain. It is hardy and gentle

Red-crested Cardinals are very common and make good aviary birds.

with suitable companions in captivity. It has not apparently been bred in captivity, though M. Decoux had birds nest in his aviaries in France in 1922 and 1923. However, no young ones were reared. It was first seen in Europe in 1877, when Miss Hagenbeck exhibited one specimen at a bird show at Hamburg.

At liberty, this bird frequents dry cactus country near the coast.

Red-crested Cardinal *(Paroaria cucullata)*

Description: Head, crest, chin and throat crimson; back, wings and tail, rich clear gray; a broad belt behind the cheeks and remainder of the underparts white; beak horn color. The hen is less pure in color, and has a narrower, more tapering beak. Length: about seven and one-half inches (190.5 mm). Habitat: south Brazil and Argentina to Bolivia.

This is the commonest of the cardinals, and is a fine aviary bird of a cheerful disposition, but not much of a songster. It will agree fairly well with the Green Cardinal, but cannot be safely associated with any of its near relations, or even with the Virginian Cardinal. It has bred fairly frequently.

The Pope Cardinal (*P. larvata*) is rather like the Red-crested, except that it is slightly smaller, lacks the crest and has a black patch on the back. The sexes are practically alike but the hen is said to be larger than the cock, with a rather longer and more tapering beak. It comes from Brazil, where it is a popular cage bird. The young birds do not attain their adult coloring until the spring of the third year. Like all the birds of this genus its notes are harsh and gritty. It would probably breed readily in a large, naturally planted aviary, if supplied with an abundance of live food. Many ornithologists regard this species as a synonym for *P. cucullata*.

The Yellow-billed Cardinal (*P. capitata*) has an intensely rich carmine head; upper parts black, the black and red being divided by snow white; throat black, the color tapering down to the chest; below pure white; beak and feet yellow. The hen has the head more brick hued and is slightly larger than the cock. Her beak is shorter and tapers more regularly. This fine bird was formerly extremely rare, but has appeared on the market in some numbers recently. It is a native of Argentina and Paraguay northwards to Bolivia and the Matto Grosso. The immature bird has been described as a separate species under the name of Brown-throated Cardinal. It is now known that the coloring of the throat, beak and feet gradually change as the birds grow older.

Green Cardinal (*Gubernatrix cristata*)

Description: Olive green above, with black streaks on the mantle; tail, bright yellow with the two middle feathers blackish; crest, chin and throat, velvety black; a broad steak over the eye, and the sides of the throat golden yellow; breast green, becoming bright yellow on the abdomen and under-tail coverts; beak black with gray lower mandible. In the hen the streak over the eye is pure white, as also are the sides of the throat; the breast is brownish gray, and the yellow coloring less vivid. Length: seven and one-half inches (190.5 mm). Habitat: Argentina to Patagonia.

120

Dr. Butler describes the song of this cardinal as consisting of, "Three rather shrill and one lower whistle, followed by a medley of scroopy struggling sounds, as though a number of different whistles were wrestling for mastery; it is not at all pretty."

Green Cardinals are excellent aviary birds.

Nevertheless, the Green Cardinal is a most popular cage and aviary bird, being much more steady than the other species, becoming perfectly tame within a very short time. It does not seem spiteful in a mixed collection, but sometimes takes objection to species wearing similar green plumage. It has been bred on a number of occasions, though successful rearing of any Cardinal in captivity is always regarded as an achievement of which the aviculturist may be proud. A hybrid between the Green and Red-crested Cardinals has been produced on at least two occasions—a remarkable cross seeing that these birds belong to different genera.

121

GROSBEAKS

The Grosbeaks *(Coccothraustes)* and Seed-eaters *(Sporophila)* vary in size from that of a thrush to that of a small waxbill. They are stoutly built, cobby birds, with roundish and rather large heads, very large powerful beaks, strong legs and rather short wings. One species is found in Britain. On the whole, they are not at all aggressive birds, but some caution should be exercised in associating them with smaller and weaker species. They are good aviary birds, many being hardy, and a number of them have been bred in captivity.

Plenty of variety is necessary in their diet, and they should have the usual seed mixture of canary, millet, wheat, sunflower, a little hemp, and a few oats. Fruit, berries, insectile mixture, and bread and milk can also be given; and of course, live insects and green food.

Hawfinch *(Coccothraustes coccothraustes)*

Description: Lores, throat, around the base of the beak black; crown and cheeks reddish brown; nape ash gray; back nut brown; wings black and greater coverts white; purplish red below. Length: seven inches (177.8 mm). Habitat: Europe.

The Hawfinch is not a rare bird, but is so shy and retiring that it is seldom seen. It is a woodland species, and has a habit of frequenting the tops of tall ash and other trees. It collects in flocks of small size in winter, and is then more often observed. Pairing takes place early, and the large, untidy nest is built of slender twigs, lined with rootlets, hair, and lichens. Three or four eggs are laid about the middle of April, and the hen bird alone incubates them.

The Hawfinch is not considered an easy bird to breed in captivity, but there is a record of its having produced a hybrid with the Bullfinch. Hawfinches are not very keen builders, and the best plan to breed them is to use old blackbirds' nests fixed up in a clump of heather or a similar shrub. These should be put on a shelf of twiggy branches around the walls of the aviary. Wicker baskets could be used, traveling boxes or even strawberry punnets lined with moss or grass. The birds are generally content to just line these nests with dry grasses. Give the birds meal worms daily, sunflower seeds, fruit tree prunings, green peas, and any weeds from the garden.

The Hawfinch is a shy bird which often takes to hiding in thick cover.

The birds generally come into breeding condition about the end of March, and the courtship is often on the rough side. It generally ends with the cock offering the hen tidbits, which she accepts with quivering wings, just like a young bird being fed. When young are hatched it is essential to give plenty of live food, as I believe I am right in saying that during the whole time the young birds are in the nest they are fed solely on live fare. When they leave the nest, the parents will begin to give them garden peas, soaked sunflower, and other seeds, as well as live food.

It is easy to distinguish the sex of this bird as the hen is of a much duller hue throughout her plumage.

As a show bird the Hawfinch is much in demand. The chief qualities of a winning specimen are richness of coloring, without muddiness, well-defined wing bars, and a large, well-shaped bib. This latter may be either thumbnail-shaped or triangular, but in either case it should be large and regular, extending some way down the throat.

Many ornithologists regard this bird as a member of the family Fringillidae.

Blue Grosbeak, or Brazilian Blue Grosbeak *(Cyanocompsa cyanea)*

Description: Deep blue; top of the head, ear region and lesser wingcoverts cobalt; breast, darker blue, merging into black on the abdomen; beak, flights and tail feathers black. The hen is brown, with the underparts brighter rusty brown. Length: five and one-half - seven inches (139.7-177.8 mm). Habitat: Brazil, Amazonia, Guiana, Venezuela, and Ecuador.

This is an excellent aviary bird, being gentle in disposition, and quickly becomes tame. It has been bred on a number of occasions, the first being by Dr. Russ the German aviculturist, in 1876. It has a rather pleasant song, like that of a robin.

Two other grosbeaks are sometimes on the market. The Mexican Blue Grosbeak *(C. parellina)* is smaller, and is deep indigo above, cobalt on the forehead, cheeks, lesser wing-coverts. The hen is earthy brown.

The Northern Blue Grosbeak *(Guiraca caerula)*, which ranges from Central America to southern United States of America, is brilliant cobalt, with the forehead, chin and lores black; the greater wing-coverts black, edged blue; median coverts chestnut. Length: about six and one-half inches (165.1 mm). This grosbeak is not a suitable companion for weaker species in an aviary, as it chases them about and pulls out their feathers. It is, however, a handsome bird for a large garden aviary containing birds of its own size and strength.

White-throated Finch *(Sporophila albigularis)*

Description: Dark slaty gray above; crown and sides of the head blackish; a narrow white line runs from the beak to the eye; underparts white, with a black band across the chest. The hen is grayish brown above and white below. Length: about four inches (101.6 mm). Habitat: eastern Brazil.

The *Sporophilae* are a group of seed-eaters mostly no larger than waxbills, generally soberly colored, but rather pleasing songsters. They are South American birds, and some kinds are very little known, none of them being too plentiful on the market. They should be fed mostly on canary and millet, and general treatment is as for waxbills. The White-throated Finch has a nice song, but is inclined to be spiteful toward other birds. It has bred in an aviary, building a simple, open, but strongly woven nest in a bush. Only one pair of these birds should inhabit the aviary, and they do not agree at all well with other members of the genus.

Guttural Finch *(S. gutturalis)*

Description: Olive green above; entire head black; wings and tail grayish brown; yellowish white below, gray on the flanks; beak silvery gray; feet grayish brown. The hen is brownish olive, yellowish below, tinged ruddy on the breast; wings and tail blackish, edged lighter; beak horn-gray. Length: about four and one-half inches (114.3 mm). Habitat: Brazil, Guiana, Peru, Ecuador, Colombia, Venezuela, and Panama.

This little finch is often kept as a cage bird in the countries it inhabits, but is not too frequently seen on the European bird markets. At liberty it goes in small flocks and feeds on grass seeds. The nest is loosely constructed of grasses and built in a bush, about four or five feet from the ground.

In captivity this species is long-lived and not so quarrelsome as some of its relatives. It has quite a pleasant song. Like most of the genus, it is subject to chills in cold weather and cannot be regarded as a hardy bird out-of-doors in northern climes. Hybrids have been reared in Germany between this and the White-throated Finch.

Reddish Finch *(S. bouvreuil)*

Description: Cinnamon red on the upper parts, darker on the lower back and rump; crown glossy black; underparts cinnamon red, richer on the flanks and undertail coverts; wing coverts black; rest of wing feathers black with brown edges; a white patch above the base of the inner primaries; upper tail coverts black, brownish tipped; beak, black; feet, blackish brown. The hen is olive-brown above, face, cheeks, throat, and foreneck ochreous buff, tinged with olive; center of breast and abdomen yellowish; flanks, olive brownish; wings brown and olive; beak, black.
Length: about three and one half to four inches (89 to 102 mm). Habitat: southern Brazil.

This is one of the smallest finches, and is a particularly charming bird, very long-lived for such a tiny mite. It is very tame by nature, and makes a delightful cage pet. The cock does not acquire its full adult plumage until the second year. It is very rarely imported to Europe, and very delicate when it does arrive. The hens are indistinguishable from the immature cocks, and it is said that they sing. When established it is not unduly delicate, but is quarrelsome in an aviary with other *Sporophilae*. It has a loud song, frequently uttered. It does not seem to have been bred in Britain, at any rate.

Jacarini Finch *(Volatinia jacarini)*

Description: Glossy blue-black, with purple reflections in certain lights; shoulders and wing-coverts white; beak, black; feet, light brown. The cock bird goes out of color at irregular periods, when it becomes speckled with buff-brown on the breast. The hen is mostly brown, ashy on the crown and black streaked on the underparts. Length: four—four and one-half inches (101.6-114.3 mm). Habitat: Central and South America.

This handsome finch was first imported to England in 1858, when the London Zoo received specimens, but it has never been easy to acquire hens, which are seldom offered on the market. It is usually amiable in disposition, and even shy in an aviary, and a suitable companion for waxbills. The Jacarini is always highly spoken of by those who have kept it, having a particularly vivacious disposition, and a sweet little song. The nuptial dance of the cock is particularly amusing. During this performance the wings and tail quiver as he pirouettes before his mate. The bird has bred in captivity, fairly frequently in Australia, and the usual site for the nest is in a thick bush growing in the aviary flight. The nest is cup-shaped, composed of fine grasses. Only two eggs seem to form the clutch, and these are pale bluish white, marked with reddish brown. Incubation takes twelve days, and the chicks remain in the nest for another twelve days. Often only one young bird is reared. They leave the nest before they can properly fly, and hide among the bushes for about a week by which time they have developed their wings. They then give the cock no peace, chasing him about and calling loudly for food.

The Jacarini Finch is very insectivorous, and will even catch flying insects. Gentles are often refused, but the birds are fond of small meal worms. The cock bird is often active late in the dusk, and on warm nights may be heard calling and flying after midnight.

Cuban Finch *(Tiaris canora)*

Description: Back, wings and tail, light olive green; forehead, face, chin, and throat enclosed in a black mask; below this is a broad crescent-shaped, lemon yellow belt extending across the lower throat from just behind the eyes; a border of black below the yellow band; rest of underparts rich dark gray; beak, black. The hen has the face and throat chocolate brown instead of black, and the crown is brownish gray. Length: about four inches (101.6 mm). Habitat: Cuba.

The Cuban Finch is a very popular aviary bird and a general favorite. It is not much bigger than a small waxbill, and is totally unlike the true grosbeaks, its exact position being a matter of dispute.

It is considered best to keep only a single pair of these birds in the same enclosure, as they are very vicious toward each other, though harmless to birds of different families. Efforts have been made in Australia to breed the birds on a colony system. It was found that if half a dozen pairs were put in an aviary together the birds had no time to concentrate on a particular bird, but in these instances the breeding was far below normal, and thus defeated the object. Where only two or three pairs were kept together, sooner or later the one male killed the others. Parents will always kill their young if they are left in the same enclosure after they have attained adult colors. It is advisable to remove them as soon as they are able to fend for themselves.

The Cuban Finch is a free breeder, and will use a covered nest box, but seems to prefer to nest in brushwood or a bush. It will breed continuously in summer, bringing off brood after brood.

The nest is a tightly woven structure with a tunnel-shaped entrance, which makes it difficult to inspect the contents. The sitting bird will leave the nest on the slightest provocation, often getting off her eggs when the aviary is merely closely approached. However, the eggs seem to hatch without any particular difficulty. The young are reared successfully without live food, but soaked, crumbled biscuits, wholemeal bread or sponge cake should be given. Seeding grass and sprouted millet should also be given. The Cuban Finch was first bred in Germany by Dr. Russ about 1880, and by Mr. L. W. Hawkins in Britain, in 1899.

Olive Finch (T. olivacea)

Description: Upper parts olive green, more yellow on the flights and tail feathers; forehead blackish; a yellow line from the base of the upper mandible passes over the eye to the ear coverts; cheeks, blackish; throat, yellowish orange; breast, blackish; rest of underparts mostly gray, washed with olive on the flanks, and buff on the abdomen; beak almost black. The hen resembles the cock, but is duller, and has no blackish about the face, and the chest is only mottled with black. Length: about four and one-half inches (114.3 mm). Habitat: Cuba, Jamaica, and Haiti.

The Olive Finch rather resembles the Cuban, and like it is a pretty aviary bird and a good breeder. It is, however, not by any means a peaceful species. It was first bred before 1880, and most aviculturists find it easy to breed, and it will even rear young in a large cage.

Though sometimes described as "Melodious" Finches, neither

Cuban nor Olive Finches have anything worth calling a song, their utterances being squeaky, grasshopper-like notes. They should be fed the usual seed mixture of canary, white, spray, and Indian millet. They also like a little fruit, especially sweet apple. They seldom eat live food, but it can be offered when they are breeding. However, they prefer green seeding millet, and this can easily be grown in summer by sowing a few rows of *Panicum* seed in rich garden soil in a sunny position. The young plants should be well watered during dry spells.

Orange Weavers are quite common and are frequently imported.

VII Weavers and Whydahs

The Weavers *(Ploceinae)* are a most important group of seed-eating birds to the aviculturist, being ideal for outdoor aviaries. They are hardy and colorful, the cocks of most species having very brilliant breeding plumage. Out of color, however, they are very sparrow-like, while the hens always wear somber garb. They are social and many kinds may be kept together, but they should not be associated with canaries or other weaker birds, as they are inclined to be spiteful.

They are inveterate nest-builders, and given some raffia, hay, and grass they will build their wonderful bag-shaped pendulant nests, but in most instances seldom breed. Weavers appear to need high temperatures for successful breeding. They are rarely bred in Europe, but Australian fanciers have been successful, especially with the Madagascar Weaver, and this should encourage fanciers who live in the warmer parts of the United States.

It is mostly the cocks that do the nest building, though sometimes the hens lend a hand. Weavers are extremely bad songsters. In size they vary from that of a Willow Wren to that of a large thrush.

Though generally looked upon as "rough stuff," the weavers are more deserving of careful study than any other group of cage and aviary birds. Their classification is constantly undergoing revision, and it is clear that there is a lot to be learned about the habits of even the more plentiful species.

Feeding is simple. All weavers, except the Dinemelli Weaver, require a seed mixture of canary and millet. Sprouted cereals, especially millet and oats, should also be offered. Green food and seeding grass, as well as egg-and-biscuit food, are valuable additions to the diet. When coming into color a mixture of dried ant's eggs and grated raw carrot makes a good food for improving the color of the cocks, which in some species is apt to be less bright under captive conditions. The rare Dinemelli Weaver is purely insectivorous and should be treated like a thrush. It is seldom seen in captivity.

If possible, weavers should have a separate aviary, where they make a most attractive display, being active, quite fearless and perfectly hardy birds. But owing to their restless habits they are apt to disturb the breeding arrangements of other birds. Generally speaking, they will agree with birds of their own size, but the Rufous-necked and allied weavers are inclined to be vicious in mixed company, and should only be associated with cardinals, starlings and the like.

Orange Bishop *(Euplectes orix franciscana)*

Description: Top and sides of the head, jet black; chin, neck, chest, back, and vent, brilliant orange-red, the feathers of the neck forming a ruff when the bird displays; rest of the underparts velvety black. The hen is tawny brown, with dark streaks to the feathers. When out of color the cock is of a similar hue. Length: five inches (127 mm). Habitat: from Senegal to the Sudan.

The Orange Bishop is one of the best-known as well as one of the most gaudy of the weavers, being regularly imported in large numbers. But it is rarely bred, the first successful English breeding being by Lord Poltimore, in 1913. It has been bred on a number of occasions in Australia. In a cage the fine, orange-red color of this bird is apt to fade to a pale tone. When kept in a naturally planted aviary, however, where it can obtain sufficient insect food, it will assume its correct rich color.

The Grenadier Weaver *(E. o. orix)* is similar to the Orange Bishop but larger (about 6 inches or 152.4 mm), and the chin as well as the top and sides of the head are black. It is not so common in captivity, and comes from South Africa. Most authorities consider it to be merely a race of the Orange Bishop. It is gregarious, living and breeding in communities in reed beds. It feeds on grain and insects at liberty, and is regarded as a serious pest to agriculture. The nest is oval in shape, slung between upright reeds, composed of strips of reed blade with but little lining. The eggs number two to four generally, and are greenish blue. It has been bred a number of times in Britain, the first being by Mr. De Quincey in 1912. Fairly frequent breedings have been made in Australia and the U.S.A. The young hatch after twelve days' incubation and leave the nest a fortnight later. The cock bird guards the nest, but the hen does all the business of feeding and rearing the young.

The Crimson-crowned Weaver *(E. hordeacea)* is of similar size, and differs only in the orange extending right over the crown to the base of the upper mandible. It comes from tropical Africa and Abyssinia. The first to breed it in England was Mr. W.T. Page, in 1919. Its habits are similar to the last species, being found in thousands among the reed beds.

The Black-bellied Weaver or Zanzibar Red Bishop *(E. nigroventris)* differs from the Crimson-crowned only in being entirely black below. It comes from a limited area of coastal East Africa and the island of Zanzibar. Not often seen in captivity, it was first bred in Germany in 1882.

Madagascar Weaver *(Foudia madagascariensis)*

Description: Bright crimson above; black centers to the feathers of the back, mantle and scapulars; lower back and above the tail crimson. Head and entire underparts also crimson. A black loral streak extends past the eye; beak, black; feet, flesh color. Hens are brown, with centers of the feathers blackish, except those on the rump. The wings and tail are blackish with pale olive margins; a well-defined light eyebrow streak and a dusky line along the upper ear-coverts, and yellowish with indistinct streaks on the flanks. Length: about five inches (127 mm). Habitat: Madagascar, Reunion, Mauritius, Seychelles.

This splendid bird is well distributed in its native land, and breeds individually, not in colonies as do so many weavers. After the breeding season, however, the birds collect in flocks and feed in the rice fields. The nest is pear-shaped, made of fine grasses, and placed in a thick bush or among reed thickets.

The Madagascar Weaver has been known to aviculture for a long time, but for many years it disappeared from the market. It was first bred in Germany during the latter part of the last century by Dr. Russ—a pioneer of modern birdkeeping. At the present time the bird is being quite freely bred in Australia and Europe. Local fanciers carefully nurse their depleted stocks of overseas finches.

Australian fanciers house their birds in aviaries with a shelter and an open, planted flight, the dimensions ranging from about

The Madagascar Weaver is a hardy bird, not normally aggressive.

ten feet by six feet to those of considerably larger size. The birds generally nest in the open flight, building in bushes, but sometimes they will use an ordinary covered finch nest box or a budgerigar box. They have been known to take to a hollow log. Once a nesting site has been chosen, the birds breed in the same spot season after season.

The eggs number from three to five and are pale blue. They hatch in a fortnight, and the birds leave the nest in another fourteen days. The cock does all the nest building, and the hen alone incubates the eggs. The hen nearly always does all the feeding of the young ones, but on one occasion when the hen died at this stage, the cock bird took over and successfully reared his family. It has been found practical to keep more than one pair of these birds in the same aviary. If a cock proves aggressive, the device of slightly clipping the flights of one wing, so that he cannot fly too well, is often successful in checking the bully. It has been found that the birds will nest up to eight times a year in Australia.

When the young birds are hatched, an abundance of live food, as well as insectile mixture, bread and milk, seeding grass, etc., must be given. Meal worms may be freely supplied.

The Madagascar Weaver is hardy in constitution and a most desirable aviary bird. A few cocks are aggressive, but the bird is not normally of a spiteful disposition.

The Comoro Weaver (*F. eminentissima*) is rather similar to the Madagascar in appearance and comes from the Comoro Islands. It is rather larger than the last species, and has a brownish olive back, instead of scarlet. It is not so desirable as an aviary bird, being inclined to be vicious, and must never be associated with any weaker birds. The Comoro Weaver is similar in habits to the Madagascar. It has been found quite easy to breed in Australia, but dangerous when nesting. After selecting a nesting site, the birds will defend a large area in the vicinity, swooping on unsuspecting companions with surprising speed. This can be checked to some degree, however, by slightly clipping the flight feathers so that the birds can still fly, but not as well as when full-flighted.

Napoleon Weaver (*Euplectes afra*)

Description: General color, rich canary yellow; cheeks and chin, black; breast, black with a yellow band across the chest; wings and tail, brown; beak, blackish; legs, flesh color. The hen is brown, streaked with darker, a buff line over the eye. The cock resembles her when out of color. Length: four and one-half inches (114.3 mm). Habitat: West Africa.

This is one of the most attractive weavers, the cock in full plumage being a splendid study in black and yellow. Dr. A.G. Butler writes: "When in colour the male is very excitable, puffs up its feathers and sings its strange song, which commences with four or five clicks and then goes off into a sort of hacking cough; the bird's plumes are also shown to great advantage in flight, which is short, jerky, abrupt, and very like a clockwork toy; between each flight, usually in pursuit of some other bird, the wings are jerked up and down over the bird in a most mechanical manner."

The Napoleon Weaver (also known as Yellow-crowned or Golden Bishop) is an excellent aviary bird, being amiable in disposition for a weaver, long-lived, and very hardy. It was first bred in England by Lord Poltimore in 1912, and on a number of occasions since. Both sexes, when out of color, can be distinguished from Orange Bishops in similar condition by the darker shade of brown and pronounced yellowish eyebrow streaks.

Closely related and also a good cage bird is the Taha Weaver *(E. taha).* It is slightly smaller and has the whole of the breast black, lacking the yellow band across the chest. It comes from South Africa, and was bred for the first time in Britain by Mr. W. Shore-Baily, who writes in *Aviculture* Vol. 1, as follows: "A neat dome-shaped nest was built in a clump of rushes, in which two eggs were laid, white lightly speckled with brown. Incubation lasted thirteen days. The hen fed the young from the start with small insects, but after a few days took meal worms and wasp grubs, which she swallowed and regurgitated. The cock did not assist its mate in the rearing operations. Nevertheless, two strong young birds left the nest in due course, one of which came into full color the following spring."

Yellow-rumped Bishop *(Euplectes capensis)*

Description: General color, rich velvety black; rump, sulphur yellow; wings, dark brown; yellow on shoulders. The hen is brown above, streaked with darker, pale brown below; chestnut on shoulders; orange on rump, heavily streaked with blackish. Length: six and one-half inches (165.1 mm). Habitat: South Africa.

This handsome weaver is common in its native land and quite often imported, as is seldom the case with South African species. It is mostly found in marshy places, where the cocks in full plumage generally perch on the topmost twigs of bushes, their black and yellow plumage being very conspicuous. Like most weavers, the nest in cleverly built among the reeds, with three or four reed stems supporting it like pillars. The hens are very shy when breeding, keeping out of sight among the reeds, with which their colors harmonize so well and in such strong contrast to the gay hues of their mates.

Opinions differ regarding the disposition of this weaver in the aviary. It has a reputation for being quarrelsome and mischievous, but Mr. Shore-Baily found it quite harmless with other birds. It

136

was bred in Germany many years ago, but does not seem to breed any more readily than other weavers, in spite of the assertion by Dr. Russ that it is the easiest of all the Fire-weavers to persuade to breed in captivity. It is very fond of insects, showing a preference for meal worms and caterpillars.

Red-billed Weaver *(Quelea quelea)*

Description: Face and chin enclosed in a black mask; rest of head, throat and breast, bright rose color, shading into brown on the back and whitish on the belly; wings and tail brown; beak, red. The hen is streaked brownish, the flights and tail feathers being edged with yellow; buff to white below; beak, waxy ochre yellow. Length: five (127 mm) inches. Habitat: West and South Africa.

Red-billed Weavers are frequently imported and are popular aviary birds.

This is one of the most frequently imported of the weavers and is a popular aviary bird, but very seldom breeds. The cock is, however, an industrious builder, and is always at work during the summer building ball-shaped nests, which he pulls to pieces again in the winter.

"When building," says Butler, "they will let no other weaver approach them, but will raise their wings almost to their heads, and use shocking language at the intruders. But when weary of this work, they rest on a branch at a short distance, and any bird may meddle with the nest with impunity, unless it so happens that the working fit comes on again whilst some meddlesome fellow is trying to discover how it is put together, when there is sure to be a charge, a chase, and much chattering, but nothing worse."

There is an aberration in which the black mask is replaced by buff, called Russ's Weaver. It was first bred in France by Mme. Lecallier in 1921, and possibly much earlier in Germany. The eggs are blue-green, three to seven in number, and hatch in fourteen days.

The Red-headed Weaver *(Q. erythrops),* from Africa, is rather scarce. It differs from the Red-billed in having the entire head crimson, becoming nearly black on the chin and throat, and the beak is blackish, lighter on the lower mandible. It has been bred in Germany, according to Dr. Russ, and in later years in Holland and England.

Rufous-necked Weaver *(Ploceus cucullatus)*

Description: Head, chin and throat, black; nape, chestnut, the color extending in a collar round the neck, bounding the black mask; shoulders, black; wings, brown, feathers broadly edged with yellow; tail, olive-brown; rest of body plumage orange yellow; beak, horn brown; eyes, reddish brown. The hen is mostly brown-and olive-streaked; the wings and tail are edged with yellow, and there is a clear, yellowish eyebrow steak. Length: about seven inches (177.8 mm). Habitat: Africa—Senegal to Abyssinia, Mozambique to Southwest Africa.

The Yellow Weavers are quite a distinct group, and some of them do not go into eclipse plumage. The cocks of the present species, for instance, assume their full colors within the first twelve months of their lives and never lose them.

The Rufous-necked Weaver is a commonly imported bird, but is somewhat large in size—about that of a Cardinal—and of a decidedly spiteful disposition. It is, therefore, best kept in a large outdoor aviary, where it makes a suitable companion for doves, parrakeets, starlings, hangnests, etc.

It is a colorful bird, as vicious as it looks, a free weaver of nests and has bred on a few occasions in captivity. In spite of its disadvantages it is a popular bird, and is both lively and interesting in habits when kept in an aviary. It keeps up a constant chattering of harsh, shrill notes, more curious than tuneful.

At liberty, this weaver is gregarious, building its retort-shaped nests in colonies in large trees, often in towns and villages. The nest is woven of grass and leaves, and the two or three eggs are pale green with a few brownish speckles.

The courting display of the cock Rufous-necked Weaver is most interesting. With neck outstretched to its fullest extent, the feathers of the neck raised, wings drooping and beak wide open, the bird hisses and grates excitedly, swaying backward and forward with a curious, slow motion. Sometimes an upside down position is assumed in which the bird sways slowly to and fro like a huge yellow butterfly. These habits are common to the genus.

Cape Weaver (*Ploceus capensis*)

Description: Head and underparts, bright golden yellow; back, olive yellow streaked with brown; wings and tail, brown, the feathers edged with yellow; lores and feathers around the eye, dusky; beak, black; feet, flesh color. The hen has the upper parts olive green; wings brownish, the coverts with whitish, and the flights with yellowish green. Sides of head, chin, throat, and breast are dark mottled buff, paler on abdomen; beak and feet, flesh color. Length: about six inches (152.4 mm). Habitat: South Africa.

This is the most golden of the group, and is altogether a very attractive bird, but not commonly imported. A pair built in the aviaries of Mr. Shore-Baily in 1916. The nest was suspended from the wire roof of the aviary and was retort-shaped and lined with feathers. Though three clutches of eggs were laid, they were all infertile. It has been successfully bred in Germany. There is a race of this bird (*P. c. olivaceous*) which differs in having a chestnut wash about the head. In this species, the cock is plain in winter, resembling the hen. In a wild state this bird is fond of nectar obtained from flowering trees, and it nests in colonies near rivers.

Half-masked Weaver *(Ploceus velatus)*

Description: Crown and lower throat, rufous; black mask encloses eye and side of the head, passing under the chin; rest of head, neck, and underparts, bright yellow; back, olive, streaked with darker; wings and tail, brownish olive, feathers edged with yellow. The cock in winter plumage is brown above, with darker streaks; olive-yellow on rump; wings, brown, margined with yellow; tail, olive; crown and nape tinged with olive-yellow; sides of the head, olive-brown with a yellow tinge; a faint yellowish eyebrow stripe; yellowish brown below, with white in the center of the abdomen. The hen differs from the winter plumage of the cock in the grayish brown color of the lower back, rump and upper-tail coverts. Length: five and one-half inches (139.7 mm). Habitat: southern Angola, north Rhodesia, southwest Africa, Natal. Represented in northeast and west Africa by a similar bird, *P. vitellinus.*

The Half-masked Weaver is one of the prettiest of the yellow species, and nests freely in aviaries, but young are not often reared. It was bred in the London Zoo, for the first time in captivity, in 1892. It is of fairly peaceful disposition, especially in a spacious aviary, and is hardy, active and an industrious weaver of kidney-shaped nests. The eggs are white to greenish, more or less spotted with reddish brown. The young are said to be fed largely on insects, and they remain in the nest for thirty days.

The Black-headed Weaver *(P. melanocephalus)* is a somewhat smaller bird from West Africa. The whole head and throat are black; upper parts, greenish yellow, and bright yellow below. The beak is blackish brown. The hen and cock out of color are yellowish green above, brownish on the crown and shoulders, each feather having a broad dull yellow transverse bar; eyebrow stripe and sides of head clear yellow; brighter yellow on the underparts. In winter plumage the cock may be distinguished from the hen by being larger in size and having a wash of gray on the cheeks; the mantle is of a more rufous shade. This weaver was first bred in England by Lord Poltimore, in 1912.

Little Masked Weaver *(Ploceus luteola)*

Description: Forehead, cheeks, ear-coverts, chin, and throat are black; rest of head, breast, and underparts, canary yellow; back, olive green, streaked; wings and tail brownish olive, and feathers edged yellow; beak, black. The female has no black in her plumage and is mostly brownish above, with a wash of yellow about the head and rump; white below, tinted with yellow. Length: about four and one-half inches (114.3 mm). Habitat: northern tropical Africa.

This is a small weaver, about the size of a Siskin and not altogether unlike that bird. It is only occasionally imported, but was bred by Mr. Shore-Baily in 1914. The birds built a nest suspended from a branch over a pond, and this was shaped like a miniature retort, the entrance hole being so small that it was impossible to insert two fingers at the same time. Two white eggs were laid, which were incubated for twelve days. The young were fed by their parents on insects, and were supplied directly with meal worms by Mr. Shore-Baily. These birds left the nest after the seventeen days and could fly strongly. Later in the season the parents went to nest again and two more young ones were reared.

Thick-billed Weaver *(Amblyospiza albifrons)*

Description: General color above, chocolate brown; lower back, rump and upper-tail coverts, blackish; wings, blackish, the primaries white at the base forming a large speculum; head and neck, chocolate brown; forehead, white; dark brownish gray below, streaked faintly with blackish; beak, black. The hen is light rufous brown above, mottled with dark brown centers to the feathers; underparts whitish, heavily streaked with dusky brown. Length: seven inches (178 mm). Habitat: southeast Africa.

This is a very uncommon and odd-looking weaver, having a powerful beak like that of a grosbeak. The hen is quite unlike the cock, having a thrush-like color scheme, and she is said to be quite a good singer. It is a rather silent bird for a weaver, and breeds in reed beds, where it builds an oval nest with a sort of porched entrance on one side, slung between two upright reeds.

Mr. Shore-Baily obtained a cock and two hens in 1924, and he says, "On turning them into my bird-room I became acquainted with the strength of their beaks. They can bite twice as hard as any of the smaller parrots and once they have got a hold, hang on like bulldogs. However, they seem harmless with other birds, as they have made no attempt to hurt the waxbills and whydahs flying with them. They seem particularly fond of the larger seeds, like saffron and sunflower."

Baya Waver *(Ploceus philippinus)*

Description: A mask of dark, blackish brown encloses the sides of the head, chin, and throat; remainder of the head and breast, bright yellow; upper parts, brownish, the feathers broadly margined with bright yellow; rump, fulvous; undertail, grayish white. The hen, as well as the cock in winter plumage, is fulvous above, streaked with blackish brown, the streaks fading out on the rump; wings and tail, brown, edged with fulvous; a clear pale eyebrow streak; throat and chin, buffish white; rest of underparts ochreous buff. Length: six inches (152.4 mm). Habitat: India, Ceylon, Burma to Malaya.

This bird is renowned for its remarkable nest, which is built like a retort with the mouth pointing downwards to the ground. Sometimes large numbers of these purse-like structures, wonderfully woven of grasses, may be seen suspended from a tree, generally a lofty palm, though they may be hung from the thatch of a bungalow. The Baya Weaver is always ready to build nests in an aviary if suitable materials are supplied. Both sexes work together, and one bird alone cannot complete a nest. The hen stays inside threading back the grasses through the walls as the cock pushes the ends through. In this way a tough, woven structure is made, almost too firmly constructed to be torn apart by hands.

The Baya Weaver is quite an attractive addition to a garden aviary, and can be associated with most birds of its own size and strength, and can even be put in with budgerigars.

WHYDAHS

These birds are very closely related to the weavers and are entirely an African group. They are most interesting birds to the aviculturist, and some of them are parasites, laying their eggs in the nests of other birds. Unfortunately, they rarely breed in captivity, and success is most likely to be achieved in a large, naturally planted aviary. Cocks in full color have magnificent tails and rich colors, but when out of plumage they are dull, sparrow-like birds. The hens are always somberly clad. A habit common to all of them is that when feeding they scratch the soil, after the manner of poultry. They have fascinating courtships, the cock rising up and down in the air above the hen, flapping his wings with a regular and noisy beat.

They are among the most easily managed of birds, requiring the same seed mixture as for weavers and waxbills, and a few insects and larvae.

Pintail Whydah (*Vidua macroura*)

Description: Crown, chin, back, a short band at the side of the chest, and tail are greenish black; a broad band of white on the wing coverts; rest of plumage is snow white; beak, coral red; eyes, dark brown. The hen is mottled brown and black above; on the head are six blackish stripes intersected by brown lines, dotted with dark brown. Length: the body is about five inches (127 mm). Tail in a fully developed cock is about twice body length. Habitat: Africa, south of the Sahara from Senegal to Eritrea, and also the islands of St. Thomas and Fernando Po.

This is a common and widely distributed whydah, and one of the most frequently imported as a cage and aviary bird. It goes in small parties, usually consisting of one male bird in full plumage and half a dozen or more hens or immature males. It is a parasite, laying its eggs in the nests of waxbills. Before laying an egg, the hen destroys one of those in the nest, after the manner of Cowbirds. The young whydahs grow up with the family of the foster parents, and remain with them for a while after becoming fully fledged. The eggs are pure white. It has been bred in captivity in large aviaries, as in 1909, when Mrs. Annington found two young ones flying in an aviary of mixed finches. Nothing was seen of their breeding, so this is perhaps an unsatisfactory record.

Unfortunately, the cock Pintail Whydah when in full dress is very vicious and spiteful in the aviary and, small though he is, should not be associated with any but rather large birds. Like all the whydahs, the Pintail is quite hardy.

143

The Pintail Whydah can be a spiteful bird and is capable of doing damage to its victims.

Long-tailed Combassou *(V. hypocherina)*

Description: Glossy steel blue; tail black; a few grayish white feathers on the flanks; white patch below wings at sides of back; beak, red; feet, dusky; eyes, dark brown. The hen is mixed brown and rufous-buff above, the lighter color edging the feathers; center of the crown reddish buff, bounded on each side by a broad black stripe from the beak to the nape; a broad white eyebrow stripe, cheeks and ear-coverts of the same color, the latter surmounted by a black streak; underparts white, washed reddish buff at the sides of the breast and abdomen; beak and feet, light brown. Length: four inches (101.6 mm). Habitat: East Africa.

This is a fine species as a cage and aviary bird, and has been imported to Europe on several occasions since 1898. It looks like a Steel Finch, but the four median tail feathers are very long and narrow. It is, however, related nearly to the Pintail Whydah, and like that bird is certainly a parasite on waxbills.

Shaft-tailed or Queen Whydah *(V. regia)*

Description: Above is black; feathers of the rump are gray at the base; wings, smoky brown; a broad tawny buff collar behind the head; ear-coverts, cheeks, and underparts, tawny buff, rufous on the flanks, where there is a large tuft of silky white plumes; under the tail, black; tail feathers, short and dark brown in color, with the exception of the four central ones which are greatly elongated, each feather being a bare shaft for the greater part of its length, and then widening toward the extremity. The hen is brown, streaked with darker above; buff on the head and neck, with a line of rufous on each side of the crown from the nostrils to nape; white and sandy below. Length: about five inches without tail (127 mm). Total length of full plumaged males is ten to thirteen inches (254-330.2 mm). Habitat: South Africa.

The Queen Whydah is found in small parties, mostly consisting of females, in thorny scrub or open, grassy places, where they search for seeds and insects on the ground. This bird is said to be a parasite upon the Violet-eared Waxbill, and its egg is white and slightly more rounded than that of the foster parent. The young are very similar to Violet-ears, even to the color of the mouth spots, but have shorter tails and lack the blue on the rump.

The Shaft-tailed or Queen Whydah makes an ideal show bird.

This handsome Whydah is much sought after by aviculturists, and is an ideal show bird, being common and the cock is generally in full color from August to December—the show season. Bachelor cocks are quite peacefully disposed toward each other and to other birds, but when associated with hens they are likely to be quarrelsome.

Red-collared Whydah *(Euplectes ardens)*

Description: General body color, jet black, with a broad crimson collar across the chest; under the tail, grayish, streaked with a darker shade; wings, black, the feathers edged with fulvous. Out of color, the cock is light buff with blackish mottling above; underparts are white stained with buff; throat tinged with red; wings are black, edged with buff; tail, black; beak and feet, black. The hen is light brown above, with blackish centers to the feathers; a well-defined yellowish streak above the eye, and a black streak behind it; underparts buff, washed with tawny on the breast, and some darker shaft-stripes; beak and feet, pale brown. Length: without the tail, about four and one-half inches. Total length of fully plumaged cock is up to fifteen inches (381 mm). Habitat: southeast and southwest Africa.

This fine whydah has been imported in small numbers and is a favorite aviary bird, having the advantage of being suitable for a mixed collection which contains budgerigars. Most aviarists find it an even-tempered bird. It is believed to be polygamous but not parasitic. The nest is built in grass or weeds a few feet from the ground, and is domed with the entrance at the side, carefully woven of fine grass, and often with growing grass stems built into the walls. Surrounding grass is plaited over the top of the nest to act as a sort of canopy and to ward off sun and rain. It has not been bred in captivity, though hybrids with other whydahs have been raised in aviaries.

Giant Whydah *(E. progne)*

Description: Jet black, glossy, like watered silk below; shoulders covered with a large patch of deep orange, relieved behind with a broad patch of buff; wings are black, edged with light brown; beak, bluish; tail consists of long, broad, curved plumes almost like a cock's tail, black in color. The hen, and the cock in winter plumage, is brown streaked and spotted with blackish; eyebrow streak, lores, and feathers encircling the eye are whitish. Length: about eight inches (203.2 mm). The tail of the cock measures up to about sixteen inches. Habitat: South Africa.

The Giant Whydah is a sociable bird, frequenting marshy places and building a nest similar to the last species. It is regularly imported and has bred in captivity several times, the first being in

England by Mr. Teschemaker, in 1909. Four eggs were laid and were incubated twelve days. The cock was shut into another aviary, so the hen reared the young unassisted. Unlimited live food was given and the young grew quickly, the first one leaving the nest when fifteen days old. The cocks of this bird look very impressive in a large aviary, where they flit about like great butterflies. It is a hardy species. Unfortunately, it goes out of color in autumn until spring, so is not suitable for show purposes. In mixed company it is one of the most amiable of the whydahs.

White-winged Whydah *(E. albonotatus)*

Description: General color black; lesser wing coverts, yellow; middle coverts edged with brownish white; beak, pale blue; feet, black. The hen is brownish above, the feather edges paler; a broad eyebrow streak and underparts buff. The cock in winter plumage is like the hen, except that the lesser wing coverts are of a brighter yellow, and the white on the wing is present as in summer. Length: about nine inches (228.6 mm). Habitat: Angola and East Africa.

This is one of the smallest of the long-tailed whydahs, the tail being only slightly longer than the wing. It is fairly often imported, and is an elegant and charming bird in an aviary. It has bred a number of times in captivity, especially in Australia. The first success in England was by Mr. Teschemaker, in 1915. The nest is built in long grass, and the eggs are greenish blue, strongly spotted with violet and brown, mostly at the larger end. There are several races of this bird, and these differ slightly with regard to wing color or length of tail.

Little is known about the home life of this lovely whydah, but it inhabits marshy ground, where, in summer, the cocks like to sit on reed-heads, showing off their glossy black plumage and conspicuous, yellow shoulder-mark. The white of the wings from which the bird takes its popular name is chiefly visible in flight. The cocks have a habit of swelling out the neck feathers into a sort of ruff and fluttering with upraised wings over the grass. It is partly insectivorous in diet.

Yellow-backed Whydah *(E. macrourus)*

Description: Jet black; mantle and shoulders are rich canary yellow; wing coverts chrome yellow. The hen is brownish gray, the feathers of the mantle being edged with yellow; underparts whitish, with darker markings on the breast. The cock in winter plumage is like the hen, but the wings are blacker and the coverts are bright yellow. Habitat: from Senegal across to the Sudan, Angola to Mozambique.

Regularly imported, the Yellow-backed Whydah is a most charming aviary bird, being peaceful in disposition, and will breed under suitable conditions. It has been bred in England. In the aviary it is not at all destructive to plants and is hardy when established. It nests in tall grasses.

The Yellow-shouldered Whydah *(E. macrocercus)* is occasionally imported from Abyssinia or Eritrea. It is rather larger than the last species and has a longer, broader tail. The back and scapulars are black. The hen is darker above than the hen of the Yellow-backed Whydah. It inhabits marshy ground and has a plaintive song.

Red-shouldered Whydah *(E. axillaris)*

Description: Glossy black; lesser wing coverts are bright orange-red; median coverts edged with the same color; beak is a bluish horn color; feet, black. The hen is mostly brown, with dark centers to the feathers above; wings and tail blackish brown, edged pale brown; brownish buff below; a broad whitish eyebrow streak. The cock in winter plumage differs from the hen in having orange-red lesser wing coverts, and black flights and tail feathers. Length: seven inches (177.8 mm). Habitat: South Africa.

This species is not often imported. It is said to be very insectivorous in a wild state. Dr. Stark writes: "Each female builds and occupies a separate nest. During the time she is sitting the male stations himself on a tall weed somewhere near the center of his harem, and keeps a sharp lookout for intruders, occasionally flying around to see how matters are progressing at his various establishments. Should a man or other dangerous enemy approach, he flies to each nest in succession with a warning note, upon which the sitting females leave their nests, creep under the grass for some yards, then rise on the wings to follow him to a distance."

The Bocage's Whydah (*E. bocagei*), is occasionally imported from Cameroons or Angola. It is a somewhat heavily built type of the Red-shouldered Whydah, but has orange instead of scarlet shoulder patches, and a larger beak. It is polygamous, and the hens build their nests in grass tufts, a few inches off the ground. They are oval and domed, beautifully light and airy, with a side entrance near the top. It has not yet been successfully bred in captivity, though a pair nested and laid two eggs in Mr. Shore-Baily's aviaries, in 1916.

Paradise Whydah *(Steganura paradisea)*

Description: Whole head black; a broad band of chestnut on the nape extends across the chest; underparts, white; wings and tail, black; beak, black; feet, brown. The tail feathers vary in length considerably, from six inches to thirteen inches or more. The hen is brown streaked above; a black line along the side of the crown, and another from the eye backward; a buff eyebrow streak; buff to white on the underparts. The cock out of color is like the hen, but is larger and of a richer shade throughout; the crown is said to be broader with the central area darker and more distinctly streaked; the eye stripe is clearer buff, and the base of the beak broader. Length: about six inches (152.4 mm) when out of color. Habitat: Africa.

This is one of the most popular of aviary birds, and the cock in full plumage is one of the most striking of common foreign birds. It is gentle in disposition, and not as restless as the Pintail Whydah. It is hardy, long-lived, harmless to either other birds or plants in the aviary. Though found nearly all over Africa very plentifully its breeding habits remain practically unknown, and the egg is undescribed. The bird parasitizes three races of the Melba Finch.

When perched the cock lets his long tail hang down, but when on the ground it is raised, the wings being at the same time slightly lowered. When flying the tail is horizontal, and it is said that these birds fly extremely high.

There are a number of races which differ chiefly in the width of the tail feathers and the shade of chestnut or golden brown around the neck. The race with the widest tail is that most often imported

A Paradise Whydah is a beautiful aviary bird.

from Senegal. *(S. p. orientalis)* The typical form *(S.p. paradisea)* comes from South Africa and is usually sold by dealers as the Golden-naped Paradise Whydah. The Paradise Whydah is hardy and easily maintained on the usual seed mixture of canary and millet. It is a suitable companion for waxbills and any other small seed eaters.

Jackson's Whydah *(Euplectes jacksoni)*

Description: General color is black and glossy; wings are dark brown, fringed with pale fawn; beak, whitish gray; feathers of the nape and upper back are very long and nearly square at the end, with a shining border; tail, with arched feathers like those of a farmyard cock, glossy black. The hen is light fawn, with distinct dark streaks, and a fawn eyebrow streak; underparts light fawn. Habitat: the high tablelands of the center and west of Kenya, and Tanzania.

This is one of the most interesting of birds, but is unfortunately rare in captivity. It has been exhibited in the London Zoo, and quite a few private aviarists own specimens. It is gregarious, building a woven nest with dry grass, and covered by the neighboring stems, which the hen interlaces to form a sort of canopy. The eggs are pale green dotted with gray and rufous. It was bred in England by Mr. Shore-Baily, two young birds leaving the nest when sixteen days old. They resembled their mother. The cock acted as a sentinel and guard, but took no part in rearing the young.

The cock of this species builds circular dancing-grounds, treading down the grass, but leaving a turf in the center. Here it executes the most extraordinary dances, turning in circles, with wings trailing, head thrown back, and jumping in the air half a dozen times or so in succession, lifting up the tail and fluttering the wings, bristling up the collar feathers, and singing an accompaniment all the while. At all times the cock in full color is a ridiculously pompous little bird—it is about the size of a sparrow—and most amusing to watch.

Senegal Combassou *(Hypochera chalybeata)*

Description: Glossy greenish black, with traces of dark brown

152

The Senegal Combassou is a short-tailed Whydah often sold under the name of Indigo Finch.

on the flights and tail feathers; beak yellowish white; feet reddish brown. The hen is brown above, the feathers having dark centers; crown with a buff stripe edged with black; sides of the head buff, brownish on the ear-coverts; underparts, light brown, whitish on the abdomen. Length: four inches (101.6 mm). Habitat: Senegal to Abyssinia.

The Combassou is a whydah which does not grow a long tail, but changes its plumage in the same way as other whydahs and most weavers. The cocks remain in full color for a long time, sometimes for more than a year. It is a very popular aviary bird, being attractive, excitable and lively, but inclined to be aggressive at times toward other birds. Its note is a chirp, and the songs a harsh spluttering chatter. It is fairly long-lived, but not quite hardy, and after October a temperature not lower than forty-five to fifty degrees Fahrenheit suits it best. Its favorite food appears to be millet and spray millet. It is often sold under the name of Indigo Finch.

At liberty it is a common bird about towns and villages, but its life-history is little known. It is supposed to be parasititc on the Fire-finch. In 1914 Mrs. Mary Boyd reported the successful rearing of a young Combassou by a pair of Cordon Bleus. She states that the hens laid their eggs in the Cordon's nest, and the Combassous took no interest in hatching or rearing.

The Combassous laid three eggs and the Cordons four, making a nest total of seven. Three hatched out, one Combassou and two Cordon Bleus. The latter were not fed but the Combassou thrived and left the nest.

The Steel Finch *(H. amauropteryx)*, which ranges from the Congo to the Cape, is often imported. It differs from the above species cheifly in having a coral red beak and feet. There are many variations in color shade of the genus *Hypochera*, and it is as yet not certain how many different species, races, or subspecies of these birds exist.

Tree Sparrow *(Passer montanus)*

Description: Crown chestnut; lores, ear-coverts and throat black; neck almost surrounded by a white collar; streaked brownish above; gray below. Length: five and one-half inches (139.7 mm). Habitat: Europe.

This bird may be described as a refined relation of the House Sparrow, but it differs in one respect in that both sexes are similarly colored. The main difference in the plumage is that in the House Sparrow the crown of the head is lead gray, and in the present species it is rich chestnut, while the white cheeks display a very conspicuous black spot or patch. It is a little smaller than the common bird and of less coarse build.

The Tree Sparrow does not seem to be of any particular interest as a cage or aviary bird, and is seldom seen on the show bench. However, it will thrive without any trouble at all on an ordinary seed mixture. For breeding it should have a covered nest box with a fairly large entrance hole, and a supply of hay. It prefers to roost in a nest box rather than on an open perch. The Desert Sparrow *(P. simplex)* is closely related to the Tree Sparrow and is occasionally imported.

Golden Sparrow *(P. luteus)*

Description: Chestnut above, shading into yellow on the rump; head, neck and under surface bright yellow; wings brownish black, lesser coverts dull yellow, the secondaries bordered with chestnut; tail brown with pale borders; beak horn color; feet pale brown. The hen has the yellow and chestnut of the upper parts replaced by pale brown; under parts buff, washed with brown on the sides of the head, neck and body. Length: about five and one-half inches (139.7 mm). Habitat: northeast Africa.

This pretty sparrow is found in flocks numbering twenty or so to more than fifty birds, and frequents open country. It is shy in disposition and when flying has a Linnet-like note. When in the trees it chirps like a House Sparrow. It is sometimes spiteful in an aviary. The Golden Sparrow was first bred by Mrs. Howard Williams in 1904.

The Arabian Golden Sparrow *(P. euchlorus)*, is bright yellow with paler wing-coverts; flight and tail feathers dark brown with pale borders. The hen is mostly brown above and buff below, with some yellow on the throat. It comes from the Somali Republic and Arabia, and has been exhibited in the London Zoo and is found only occasionally in dealer's cages. Both these birds do well on a seed mixture of millet, canary, hemp and oats, with a little soft food and a few insects.

VIII Waxbills

The Waxbills *(Estrildinae)* are a group of small, graceful, attractively colored finches, most of which are African, but a few are found in Asia and one in Australia. They are among the most popular of all foreign birds, having a fascination all their own.

They are delicate when newly imported, and should be kept in a warm room—one facing south for preference—for a few weeks to settle down. But once established, most of the commonly imported kinds have proved quite hardy in a snug, well-built outdoor aviary. The main difficulty is that in the short days of winter they cannot obtain enough food and suffer from the long hours of darkness. It is, therefore, strongly advisable to provide light enough for the birds to feed during winter evenings. Where a large number of waxbills are kept, it is a good plan to fit a shelf about a foot below the roof in a corner of the sleeping quarters and fill this space with suitable pieces of shrubs—heather is a good kind where available—and some hay. This makes a good sleeping place, where the little birds can huddle together and keep warm.

Waxbills live equally well in cages or aviaries, but are far happier and more interesting in the latter. The aviary should have three-eighths inch mesh netting if it is possible to obtain this, rather than the usual one-half inch. The smaller mesh prevents mice getting in. These creatures are a great nuisance in a waxbill aviary, destroying the nests, eating and fouling the seed.

Waxbills require much the same food as advised for grass-finches, but on the whole are much more insectivorous. The staple seed mixture should consist of equal parts white and Indian millet, and one-fourth part canary seed. Plenty of spray millet *(Panicum)* should be given, as well as bunches of seeding grass, chickweed, groundsel, etc. These little birds should always have bathing facilities provided, as they are keen on splashing about in a shallow dish of water. Earthenware water containers sold by hardware stores for keeping potted plants moist are ideal and can be obtained in various sizes. The handy man could make a shallow bath of cement where these birds are kept in an oudoor aviary. Incidentally, water left in the sunshine soon becomes covered with green algae—a kind of slimy plant life. This is unsightly, but not in the least harmful to the birds.

Many species of waxbills have been bred both in cages and aviaries. They require covered nest boxes, either wooden ones as provided for budgerigars or those made of rush or coconuts. In large, naturally planted aviaries they will build domed nests in bushes. There are innumerable suitable shrubs for such an aviary, but privet, cotoneaster euonymus, juniper, box and pyracantha are favorites. Honeysuckle is a good climber to plant; the flowers are attractive to insects and so provide a little live food. In a large garden aviary the parent birds will catch quite a number of insects with which to feed their offspring, but birds with young should always be offered good quality soft-bill mixture and live ant's eggs whenever obtainable. Waxbills feed their young on insect fare, not on predigested seed as do the grass-finches and mannikins. Egg and biscuit food as supplied for rearing canaries, with the addition of ant's eggs (sold as fish food), makes a useful rearing food. A supply of gentles is an essential, except in warm climates where white ants can be obtained. Gentles are the maggots of the blowfly (bluebottle), and can be bred by placing a piece of meat away with a few female flies. A tray of bran should be placed under the meat so that the maggots may fall into it and clean themselves. For town fanciers, it may be mentioned that gentles can be purchased from dealers in angling requisites, even in winter, as they are much in demand for bait. Small meal worms can be given, but in limited amounts only. A spray of rose, broadbean, or some other non-poisonous plant covered with aphids (greenfly and blackfly), is always appreciated by these feathered mites.

Waxbills are very sociable and display great affection for one another. For this reason they are usually kept in pairs, and generally many pairs occupy the same cage or aviary. But do not overcrowd them, even if you do not hope for any breeding successes.

Cordon Bleu *(Uraeginthus bengalus)*
Description: Mouse-brown above; cheeks, throat, flanks, breast, and upper tail-coverts, bright sky blue; a large crimson patch on the ear-coverts; abdomen, whitish brown; tail, dull Prussian blue.

A pair of Cordon Bleus. They are lively birds once they are acclimatized.

The hen may be distinguished by the absence of the red ear-patch. Length: four and one-half inches (114.3 mm). Habitat: east Africa, in different races.

This charming and beautiful little waxbill is a great favorite with fanciers, being a lively little bird, a good mixer in the aviary, and a fairly free breeder. The main trouble is getting imported specimens acclimatized, since this species is undoubtedly delicate in constitution when it first arrives in our colder climate. Newly imported birds should be caged in a warm room and kept at a fairly steady temperature, and not be turned out into a garden aviary until early summer. With aviary bred birds one need not take this trouble, since such are reasonably hardy, and even imported birds have wintered successfully in an outdoor aviary without heat in the south of England.

Cordon Bleus will breed when about six months old, and it is their natural inclination to breed all the year round. But this can only be allowed by fanciers living in warm countries, and those in northern climes must discourage the breeding of Cordons except in warm summer weather, otherwise hens will almost certainly succumb to egg-binding.

Cordons build a somewhat frail nest of fine grasses and will use feathers to line it if available. The usual clutch of eggs is four and the incubation period about a fortnight. The young birds are ready to leave the nest at sixteen to eighteen days. The cocks attain their full colors when about five months old.

The diet for breeding pairs must contain insect food. Cordons are very fond of the aphids that collect on beans, roses, and other plants in summer. They will also pick up minute insects from newly turned soil. Ant's eggs are excellent food, and in regions where termites are found these may also be given freely. Spray millet and seeding heads of grasses must be supplied regularly. Not more than one pair should be in the same aviary for the most satisfactory breeding results, and they are best not associated with the Blue-breasted Waxbill. They are not spiteful toward other inmates of the enclosure, but will defend their nest vigorously against intruders.

Blue-breasted Waxbill *(U. angolensis)*

Description: Similar to the Cordon Bleu, but lacks the red ear-patch and the blue is brighter in tone. Upper plumage and sides of the cheeks gray; throat, cheeks and chest light blue; abdomen and rump pale grayish white; tail, dark blue. In the hen the blue extends to the breast only, the rest of the underparts being creamy white. It is hard to distinguish the hens of this species from those of the last, but usually the beak is of a brighter pink in the Cordon Bleu. Immature birds resemble the adult female. Length: four and one-half inches (114.3 mm). Habitat: Africa, from Angola and Tanganyika southward to the Orange River on the west and Natal on the east.

This dainty little waxbill is less common in captivity than the Cordon Bleu, but is fairly plentiful in its native land. Their natural habitat is light scrub country, and they are especially fond of scattered acacia bushes, which affords them a refuge if disturb-

The Blue-Breasted Waxbill is a more hardy bird than the Cordon Bleu and is a free breeder.

ed when feeding on grass seeds. In the spring both sexes have a not unpleasant song, and the normal alarm note is a shrill twittering.

The nest is built in low bushes, from three to eight feet in height, and is a ball of grasses with a small side entrance and lined with fine grass and feathers. Three or four rather rounded white eggs are laid.

The Blue-breasted Waxbill is most desirable as an aviary bird, being much more readily established than the Cordon Bleu and hardier, besides being a free breeder. The young are fed on insect fare. In a mixed collection this species is inclined to be antagonistic only toward the Cordon Bleu, and seldom fights other birds unless attacked, at which time they are able to put most birds of their own size to rout.

Violet-eared Waxbill *(U. granatina)*

Description: General body color very rich chestnut; wings, grayish brown, with reddish margins; forehead, blue; chin and throat, black; tail-coverts, bright blue; tail, black, the feathers being blue-edged; vent is blackish; beak, purple, red at tip; legs purple-gray; eyes, red. The hen is a little duller, though hardly less beautiful, being more grayish on the upper parts, and yellower below. The throat is whitish; the violet ear-patch of the cock being replaced by lilac, and the blue of the under-tail parts is absent. Length: five and one-half inches (139.7 mm). Habitat: South Africa, to the Zambesi on the east and to Angola on the west.

Most fanciers consider this to be the finest and most beautiful of all the waxbills. It was first imported about 1890, when five specimens were presented to the London Zoo. It has been known on the continent of Europe for a much longer time, and was first brought to Europe in 1754. It has never been common, though small numbers arrive fairly regularly on the market. It is, however, always a rather costly species.

Unfortunately, this lovely waxbill is rather difficult to keep and will not survive in a temperature below fifty degrees. The usual practice in England is to keep the birds in an outdoor aviary in summer, and indoors in winter at living room temperature, i.e. fifty-five to sixty degrees Fahrenheit. It should be remembered that this bird is very insectivorous and is also very fond of grass seeds. Food should be yellow and white millet, spray millet, and a little small canary seed. Insects and small larvae as well as small spiders and gentles should be regularly supplied. It is an ideal exhibition bird.

In a wild state the Violet-eared is something of a desert dweller, inhabiting thorny scrub country, and is even found in parts of the Kalahari Desert. The nest is globular, with a side entrance, made of grasses. It is usually built in a thorn bush from three to six feet from the ground.

Though a number of near successes were achieved over a long period of time, the Violet-eared was not bred successfully until 1936, when Mrs. K. Drake of Mylor, Cornwall, reared two birds, which lived to be independent of their parents. Unfortunately, they were killed by their parents when eight weeks old. The Avicultural Society's medal was awarded to Mrs. Drake for this first breeding record. The following year, Mrs. Drake again had two young ones leave the nest.

Red-eared Waxbill *(Estrilda troglodytes)*

Description: Upper parts and wings are mousebrown, very faintly tinted with gray on the head; a crimson line from the base of the beak through the eye backward to the ear-coverts; tail, jet black; throat, whitish, very delicately tinted with pink; rest of the underparts very pale grayish white, strongly tinted with clear, carmine pinkish color; beak, waxy scarlet. Sexes alike. Length: four inches (101.6 mm). Habitat: from West African coast across the Sudan.

This species is the waxbill most commonly imported, and though an active little bird and fairly hardy as an aviary inmate, it has only been bred on very few occasions. It not infrequently builds a nest and lays eggs, but rarely progresses any further. It seems more ready to hybridize, however, and crosses between this and the Orange-cheeked, St. Helena, Crimson-rumped, and Gold-breasted Waxbills have been produced abroad, as well as with the Fire-finch.

St. Helena Waxbill *(E. astrild)*

Description: Upper parts are mouse-brown, distinctly barred with narrow transverse dark lines; underparts are washed with rose pink, which deepens into carmine on the abdomen, where it is finely barred; under tail-coverts, black; a crimson streak from the base of the beak to the ear-coverts, enclosing the eye. Beak red. The hen is a little smaller than the cock and shorter in the tail, with lighter markings, and has less pink on the abdomen. The band over the eye is shorter and the beak is more orange than red. The dark feathers under the tail are more brown than black, and less extensive. Length: four and one-half inches (114.3 mm). Habitat: South Africa, ranging to Damaraland on the west and

The St. Helena Waxbill is the largest of its genus.

Matebeleland on the east. Introduced into Madagascar, Mauritius, and St. Helena.

The St. Helena may be described as a more strongly marked edition of the last species, but is larger and with dark feathers under the tail. It is one of the most popular of the family, being hardy and a fairly free breeder. Though not normally quarrelsome, a pair inclined to nest can prove rather aggressive and may attack other birds which encroach on their nesting site. Generally speaking, most aviarists grossly overcrowd their waxbill aviaries. Though these birds are such small creatures, they need a reasonable amount of space.

Like the other waxbills, the St. Helena will use a covered nest box, or construct a spherical nest in a bush. The nest is made of interwoven grasses and has a bottle-neck side entrance. Feathers are used in quantity as a lining. The birds do not like any interference with their nest, and will desert rather readily.

In courting, the cock performs a curious kind of dance, jumping up and down, holding a piece of straw in his beak to attract his mate. The usual clutch of eggs is five, and the incubation period of about thirteen days, both birds sharing the task of incubation.

The young birds have white nodules at the base of the beak to enable their parents to see their mouths when feeding. The young birds leave the nest well feathered and at about three weeks of age. A fortnight or so later they become independent. In an aviary not overcrowded and of reasonably large size, more than one pair of St. Helenas will usually agree. The hens are somewhat subject to egg-binding if allowed to nest during inclement weather.

When breeding, the birds should be supplied with millet spray, soaked for a day or so, plenty of live ant's eggs, chopped meal worms, houseflies, gentles, and even very small earthworms. Cuttlefish bone should be available, and the birds have been known to carry small pieces of this to the nest, for what particular reason is not known. Seeding grass and chickweed, etc., should also be supplied.

Black-cheeked Waxbill *(E. erythronotos)*

Description: Head, breast, and upper back are pinkish brown; cheeks, black; lower part of the body above and below is crimson; tail, black; wings barred with gray and brown. The hen is similar but slightly smaller. Length: four and one-half inches. (114.3 mm). Habitat: South Africa.

This pretty waxbill is on the market from time to time in small numbers, and has been bred in Europe as early as 1936. It has also nested in aviaries in South Africa. Unfortunately, it is decidedly delicate until acclimatized. It is an insectivorous species, and requires a plentiful supply of live food, especially ant's eggs.

Lavender Finch *(Lagonosticta caerulescens)*

Description: Pearly gray above, lower back and tail-coverts bright crimson; two central tail feathers, dull reddish, and the remainder black; a black line from the base of the beak passes

The Black-cheeked Waxbill is insectivorous and is quite delicate until acclimatized.

through the eye; cheeks and throat, grayish white, deepening into sooty gray on the abdomen; small white spots on the flanks; beak black, with lateral red streak. The hen is a paler gray under the tail. Young birds do not have the white spots on the flanks. Length: four and one-half inches (114.3 mm). Habitat: West Africa.

This is a particularly charming little member of the waxbill family—a delightful pearly gray bird with a crimson rump and tail. Though commonly imported it is perhaps the most delicate of the waxbills when newly arrived, as may be expected seeing it comes from tropical west Africa. But the real reason for the difficulty in establishing it in captivity is that on the voyage the birds are fed only on seed, whereas this is mainly an insectivorous species. It should always be given a certain amount of insectivorous food, natural and artificial, besides the usual mixture of canary and millet seed. Small meal worms, spiders, and small larvae are much appreciated, as well as greenfly. For green food, chickweed and flowering grass—especially poa annua—are most useful.

Lavender Finches are active birds and delightful as aviary occupants, but cannot be considered at all easy to breed. The species was bred in England in 1900 by Miss Rosie Alderson. Her pair built in a cigar box and again among some pine branches, constructing their nests of grasses, dead chickweed, and other pieces of vegetation, using feathers as a lining. After a number of futile attempts a single nestling left the nest late in the year.

Lavender Finches should be wintered indoors at living room temperature, but they are better off in a garden aviary during the warmer months. A true pair in good fettle should do well on the show bench.

Lavender Finches will live on very good terms with other small finches in an aviary, but they will not tolerate the presence of others of their own kind, and it is unwise to keep more than one pair together in the same enclosure. Hybrids with the Fire-finch and Gray Waxbill are said to have been raised.

There are several sub-species of this bird, as the Black-tailed Lavender Finch *(L. c. incana)* which occurs in Congo, Angola, Nyasa and Tanganyika. It is sometimes called Perrein's Waxbill. Treatment would be similar to that advised for the common Lavender Finch.

Red-browed or Sydney Waxbill *(Aegintha temporalis)*

Description: Back and wings are dull olive; rump and upper-tail coverts, crimson; tail, dusky brown; crown, nape, cheeks, and sides of the body, gray; a rather broad crimson streak runs from the base of the upper mandible over the eye to the sides of the napes; underparts, whitish gray, more or less washed with buff; beak, crimson and black; feet, flesh color. Sexes alike. Length: four inches (101.6 mm). Immature birds are dusky, olive green above, ash gray on the head and wings. The underparts are smoky brown, crimson above the tail, and the beak all black. Habitat: eastern Australia (Cape York to South Australia).

This is a common and widely distributed bird in Australia, being found in rather thick scrub, especially in hill districts and along the sides of streams. They are usually found in flocks,

166

The Red-browed Waxbill (also called Sydney Waxbill) is more comfortable in small planted aviaries than in larger ones.

sometimes fairly large ones, and a number of nests can often be found built quite close together.

This pretty waxbill has been known as a cage bird in Europe and the United States for a long time, but it is seldom either cheap or plentiful. The reason is probably because the birds are bad travelers and do not stand up to long sea voyages at all well. In their native land they are readily obtainable for the equivalent of about a dollar a pair. It is rather short-lived as an aviary bird, but

167

breeds moderately well, though liable to desert its eggs if the nest is unduly interfered with.

It prefers to build in a thick, evergreen bush, but will also make use of the covered nest boxes. The nest is often used as a roosting place for some time before any eggs appear. The normal clutch consists of four or five eggs; when very large numbers are laid, most of them prove infertile. Incubation takes about a fortnight, and the young birds remain in the nest an additional twenty-one days. The parent birds will attack any intruders venturing too close to the nest when the young are hatched, but at other times they are very docile.

Young have been reared without live food, but in this case seeding grasses, sprouted seed, lettuce, thistles, and garden weeds were given regularly. Some spray millet *(Panicum)* was also supplied. Oystershell grit, cuttlefish, and rock salt were available.

The Sydney Waxbill was first bred in Germany at the end of the last century by Dr. Russ, and in England the first breeding was by Mr. Reginald Phillips in 1902.

Though normally not an offensive bird in mixed company, some individuals are a bit spiteful at feeding times, driving other birds away from the seed dish. It is delicate when first imported, and not too hardy in the English climate. It is a very interesting and lively bird in a garden aviary, and during courtship the cock executes a curious mating dance, hopping around the hen of his choice with his tail held obliquely sideways.

In north Queensland there is a pretty sub-species called the Lesser Red-browed Waxbill *(A. t. minor)* which has a golden olive back, white ear-coverts, and black under the tail. It measures only three and three-fourth inches. This race is practically unknown to aviculture, and only a few specimens are in the hands of Australian fanciers.

Gold-breasted Waxbill *(Amandava subflava)*

Description: Olive-brown above; rump, red; bright yellow below, fiery orange on the breast; beak and a streak passing through the eye, coral red; the hen is duller, especially on the underparts. Length: about three and one-half inches (88.9 mm). Habitat: northern tropical Africa, south of the Sahara.

This is one of the smallest and prettiest of foreign seed eaters, and is highly popular as a cage and aviary bird. In spite of its lack of size it is hardy when acclimatized, and has been known to live eight or nine years in captivity. It can be wintered out of doors without heat in the southern counties of England, but a watch should be kept on the birds to see that they are not showing signs of distress during cold spells. Shivering and drooping wings are a bad sign, and in such cases the birds should be removed to warmer quarters, or heat provided in the aviary shelter.

The Gold-breasted Waxbill is quite harmless in a mixed collection and a fairly good breeder, but it is not always easy to rear the young birds to a fully adult age. Possibly the first breeder was Dr. Russ, whose pair nested seven times with seven failures and in an eighth attempt young were hatched. In England early breedings were those by Lady Dunleath in 1904 and Teschemaker in 1905. The species is bred regularly by Australian and American aviculturists.

The birds will avail themselves of the usual, covered, finch nest box, stuffed with hay. They will line the box with feathers, which should be scattered about the aviary floor for this purpose. Hybrids have been bred between this bird and the Avadavat, Firefinch and St. Helena Waxbill. This bird is also called the Orange-breasted Waxbill.

At liberty this waxbill frequents the borders of streams and swamps, where there is a good growth of reeds, and appears to be rather shy in its habits, not allowing a close approach. In captivity, on the other hand, it is very tame. The South African race lacks any red coloring on the breast.

Orange-cheeked Waxbill *(Estrilda melpoda)*

Description: Crown, light gray; back and wings, mouse brown; underparts, whitish; rump, bright orange-red; tail, black; cheeks, orange; beak, red. The hen is slightly duller. Length: four inches (101.6 mm). Habitat: West Africa, eastwards as far as Zambia.

Orange-cheeked Waxbills are commonly imported and are favorite birds with beginners. They have much to commend them, being pretty, though not gaudy, inexpensive and quite hardy in all southern counties of England, and similar climates. The usual plan is to keep any newly-purchased birds indoors if bought in winter, and turn them outside in May. As breeders Orange-cheeked Waxbills are fairly prolific, and the best results are obtained in outdoor aviaries with planted flights, where the birds will build in a shrub or creeper about four feet from the ground. The nest is constructed of grass, and they like feathers or teased cotton wool as lining material. The birds will also make use of a finch nesting box. Four or five eggs are laid and incubation takes about fourteen days. When rearing young give a plentiful supply of small live insects, aphids, small meal worms, ant's eggs, chopped hard-boiled egg, and some slightly moistened sponge cake.

A difficulty for breeders is sexing the birds, as they are colored alike. Hens generally have rather less orange about the cheeks and of smaller area, but this is variable. Once Orange-cheeks breed they are devoted parents and work hard to satisfy the food requirements of their brood. Young birds are dull replicas of their parents, and do not assume the full plumage until after the first molt.

Experiments have proved that Orange-cheeks are good stayers at liberty. Some fanciers have let the birds out of their aviary and the birds will hunt for insects in the garden, returning to their aviary to sleep at night.

Red Avadavat or Tiger Finch *(Amandava amandava)*

Description: Upper parts of the head and back are deep mahogany brown; sides of the head, throat, and underparts, scarlet; tail, black; flanks, wings and tail-coverts covered with numerous white spots; rump, scarlet; beak, bright red; feet, pink. The hen, and the cock when in undress plumage, are alike, being reddish brown above, with white spots on the wings; upper tail coverts red; throat, breast and underparts, yellowish gray. Length: four inches (101.6 mm). Habitat: India, China, Siam, and Java. Several races.

The Avadavat differs from all other waxbills in having a seasonal change of plumage, normally being out of color from December until March. The cock in his bright scarlet breeding plumage is a striking little bird, but the process of changing color

Red Avadavats are frequently trapped in their native India, where the males are caged as songbirds. In this lovely pair, the male is the lower bird.

is somewhat slow. It is a first-rate cage or aviary bird and a fairly free breeder. The clutch varies from six to eight, but more often only four eggs are laid in captivity. It likes to line its nest with feathers, cotton-wool, down, etc. When courting, the cock dances around the hen with head erect, crown feathers raised, tail spread like a fan, and uttering his pleasant little song. It is hardy when acclimatized.

Green Avadavat (A. formosa)

Description: Olive green above, more golden on the rump and upper tail-coverts; tail, black; underparts, lemon yellow, paler on the throat; flanks banded with dark green and white; beak, red; legs, flesh color. The hen is rather like the cock, but duller above. Her chin, throat, and breast are more of a grayish hue, and only slightly tinged with pale yellow. The bill, waxy red in the cock, is less bright in the hen. Young birds are brownish above, ochreous beneath and pale buff on the flanks and sides. They lack the characteristic dark bars of the adult, and the bill at this stage is dark colored. Length: four inches (101.6 mm). Habitat: central India.

At liberty this attractive little bird frequents dense jungle grass and sugar cane fields, frequently using strips of the cane leaves to construct its large globular nest.

The Green Avadavat is easily recognized by its conspicuous blackish green and white vertical stripes which border the flanks. These, together with the gay, yellow plumage and red beak, make it a most attractive aviary bird. It is quite hardy when once acclimatized, is most entertaining in ways and not a difficult species to breed.

When courting the cock sings a one-note song, at the end of which he tilts his head backwards, then at full stretch brings it round in an arc as low as the perch, with beak wide open, as if he intended to regurgitate. A very low-pitched gurgling sound is heard. Sometimes the pair face one another on the ground, nodding their heads and circling around each other with their tails almost at right angles to their bodies.

This species was first bred by Mr. W.E. Teschemaker in 1905 and 1906. It has since been bred quite a number of times, in England as well as in the U.S.A.

The Green Avadavat is a delicate bird even when acclimatized and should be brought in for the winter.

Newly imported birds should be kept warm at first, and in any
case should not be put outside until late in May. In winter they are
most comfortable if kept at temperatures from fifty-five to sixty-
five degrees Fahrenheit.

Feeding is simple, the birds eating mostly white and spray
millet, with a little canary seed. They will nibble turf and small
seeding grasses, but are not much interested in other green food.
They are very fond of small maggots, spiders, and live ant's eggs.
Sprouted millet is a good food, especially for birds which do not
have access to a naturally planted open flight.

Fire-finch *(Lagonosticta senegala)*

Description: Entire plumage, dull crimson, except the wings and tail, which are light brown; a number of tiny white spots along the sides of the breast; beak, red. Eyelids, yellow; iris, dark brown. The hen is mouse-brown, paler below, with a crimson mask in front of the eye. Upper-tail coverts, reddish; tail, brown with crimson at the edges of the feathers. A few white spots on the sides of the breast. Immature birds are like the hen. Young cocks soon reveal red feathers, but if only a red streak appears in front of the eye, and small white spots appear on the flanks, with no other red feathers, the bird is a hen. Length: about three and one-half inches (89 mm). Habitat: from the west coast to the east coast of Africa, south of the Sahara and down to South Africa.

This is one of the most popular of the waxbills, but newly imported birds are very delicate. However, when properly established it is not a difficult bird to breed. Birds received in winter should be kept at about sixty degrees in a cage. Established birds housed in garden aviaries are fairly free breeders. The nest is mostly built by the efforts of the cock bird, and he will use a finch nest box or brushwood in the aviary shelter. Three to four eggs are laid, incubation being shared by both birds. The young birds are independent when about a month old.

When rearing, the birds require seeding grasses, any insects available, live ant's eggs, gentles, aphids and sprouted seed. Pieces of sponge cake can be offered. Many successful breeders with large, open flights place a tin of rotten fruit or horse dung in the aviary to attract small insects, which these little finches will quickly secure. In cold spells the hen must be carefully watched when about to lay, as these birds are somewhat prone to egg-binding.

Fire-finches are not very long-lived birds, about three or four years being their average allotted span. They generally agree with other small birds, but some cocks may prove vicious to others of their own kind. One pair to an enclosure is the best rule.

Fire-finches were first bred in Britain by the Rev. C.D. Farrar, who bought acclimatized birds in the summer of 1897, wintered them in a cold indoor aviary, and bred one young bird in the summer of 1898. It was bred in Germany at an earlier period.

Jameson's Fire-finch *(Lagonosticta jamesoni)*

Description: Brown above, tinged with pink; cheeks and underparts, pale pink; a few white spots on the flanks; abdomen and vent, black; tail, black, fringed with crimson. The hen is paler. Length: about four inches (101.6 mm). Habitat: South Africa and Rhodesia.

This pretty little bird has always been difficult to obtain in England and the United States, though it is much better known on the continent of Europe. It was bred in France in 1928, and for the first time in England (Kent) by Mr. F. Johnson.

The pair was put into a secluded aviary and went to nest without delay, building in a nest box near a window in their sleeping quarters. The nest box was of the all-wire type, with an entrance in the side. This the birds filled with the short pieces of hay and cow hair provided. The first egg was laid on August 27, 1935, and another in due course. Mr. Johnson wisely did not disturb the birds until September 13, when he found two chicks had hatched, and both were alive. Soaked millet seed was supplied and also live ant's cocoons dug up from paddocks. The latter were never touched, and the chicks were fed entirely on soaked seed. At the end of seven days Mr. Johnson inspected the nest, and found it contained only one chick, nearly half-fledged. The body of the other was found on the aviary floor, its pin-feathers just showing through. The remaining youngster continued to thrive and was seen off the nest September 29.

In an aviary Jameson's Fire-finch is inclined to be retiring, and hides among branches. The cock has a most delightful little song and, as one fortunate owner of a pair tells us, "few birds can look more attractive than a cock Jameson's sitting on a lofty twig in bright sunshine, chest out, and throat pulsating, trilling his sweet song and looking like a glistening ball of fiery red."

Peter's Twinspot *(Hypargos niveoguttatus)*

Description: Crown and nape, dark gray; back, umber brown, tinted with crimson; wings, darker; rump and upper tail coverts, bright crimson, as well as the middle tail feathers; black on inner webs, crimson on outer webs; face, throat, and chest, deep crimson; rest of underparts, black, spotted mainly on the flanks with

175

large round white spots; beak, slate-black; feet, reddish brown. The hen has the head gray, throat and chest orange; below, dark gray with white spots on the flanks. Length: four and one-half inches (114.3 mm). Habitat: East Africa.

This magnificent finch frequents dense bush and thorn tangles on river banks, and spends most of its time on the ground among thick undergrowth.

It is rarely on the market, but is an excellent aviary bird, of hardy constitution. It was first bred in captivity by A. Voigt, who reared young in Germany in 1928. The first breeder in Britain was Mrs. K. Drake, of Cornwall, who reared young in 1935. Her pair was housed in an aviary eighteen feet by six feet and about nine feet high, the shelter taking up some four feet, and the flight being planted out as a small garden. The birds built inside the shelter in an ovate-shaped basket nest, with an opening half way up, and later a second nest was built in the open flight, on the ground under a bush. Each nest produced four young, which were all reared. Incubation of the eggs took fourteen days, and the young remained in the nest until the age of eighteen to twenty-one days. They had brownish feathering with a decided reddish tinge showing on the tail and breast, also white warts on each side of the beak. In a very short time the characteristic spots appeared, and it was not long before the youngsters resembled their parents.

Mrs. Drake fed the birds on Indian and spray millet (*Panicum*) with a little canary seed. For feeding the chicks she offered the birds egg-and-biscuit food, a soft-bill mixture as used for delicate insectivorous species. In addition a few meal worms were taken, but Peter's do not eat these so readily as other waxbills.

A pair of Rosy Twinspots *(H. margaritatus)* were exhibited at bird shows in 1934. It is occasionally available.

Melba Finch *(Pytilia melba)*

Description: Forehead, chin, and throat, bright scarlet; rest of the head and nape, gray; back and wings, olive green; tail, blackish, crimson tinted, lighter at the base; chest, golden olive; underparts, dark gray, streaked and spotted with white; beak, scarlet; feet, pale brown. The hen is duller, the scarlet of the face being replaced by ashy gray; throat, pale gray, streaked with white. Length: five inches (127 mm). Habitat: Africa.

The Melba Finch is a commonly imported species and is a very desirable bird, and once acclimatized is a fairly hardy species, but better given some artificial heat during the colder months of the year. The cock has a not unpleasant song.

It is unfortunate that this species is very difficult to breed in captivity, since aviary-bred specimens are not only hardy but delightfully tame and charming birds.

The Melba has been bred regularly in Australia for some years past, the young being reared on supplies of termites or "white ants." It was first bred in the Isle of Wright in 1915 and in Germany in 1927. The first Australian record was in Adelaide in 1935. Some pairs of Melbas have proved ready breeders, whereas others, apparently just as fit, refuse to nest.

The nest is domed, loosely made of dried grass and lined with feathers. It is generally built in a thick bush or shrub. The eggs are white, and the usual clutch is four. Incubation lasts about thirteen days, and both birds share the task of sitting. The chicks when first hatched are dark-skinned creatures, covered with down, and showing white gaps. The immature plumage is mainly olive above and grayish green below. Rump and lower tail feathers are red, and the beak black.

It is essential to supply live food when Melbas have young in the nest, and for this purpose a supply of gentles might be the most useful stand-by. Live ant's eggs, a few meal worms and any garden insects which can be secured can be offered. If live food is withheld, the parents will usually throw the young out of the nest. The young birds should be separated from their parents as soon as they become independent, and only one pair should be in the same enclosure.

The Red-faced Waxbill or Orange-winged Pytilia (*Pytilia afra*), is closely allied to the Melba Finch and is more easily bred, but is not commonly imported. It is an attractive bird with the crown and back of golden olive, tinted reddish on the rump; face, forehead, and upper throat are red; buff below, barred with dark gray; tail, dark crimson, outer feathers, black. The hen has a gray face. Length: four and one-half inches (114.3 mm). Habitat: east Africa from the Sudan down to Mozambique and across to Angola.

Aurora Finch (*Pytilia phoenicoptera*)

Description: Ashy gray above, lighter on the head, with streaks of dark gray; wings, rump and upper tail-coverts, crimson; tail has central feathers crimson remainder blackish, edged with crimson; underparts gray, barred with white; beak, black. The hen is duller, with less crimson; underparts more distinctly and broadly barred with white. Length: four and one-half inches (114.3 mm). Habitat: west Africa.

The Aurora Finch is a striking bird, about the size of a Redpoll, rich gray with red wings and tail, and a black beak. Sometimes called the Crimson-winged Waxbill, it is a big bird for a waxbill, and more like a large Lavender Finch. It does not have much of a song, but utters a peculiar little flute-like phrase of three notes, the middle one being vibrant and prolonged. It is not nervous in disposition, but likes to hide among bushes in a naturally planted aviary—and this is the ideal place to breed it.

The Aurora Finch was first bred by Dr. Russ in Germany during the latter part of the last century, and is not regarded as an especially difficult species in this respect.

In a suitable aviary most pairs—especially aviary-bred ones—will start nesting as soon as they have had time to settle down. But results are often erratic. Some pairs will rear their young for a week or so, then leave them and start nesting again. Meal worms should be given very sparingly, as they are very stimulating. It is not very easy to rear Auroras without live food, and a regular supply of gentles (maggots of the blowfly) should be given for the best results.

Auroras are not particular as to the site of their nest, but will build in a bush, dead brushwood, or a nest box. The nest is of the typical dome-shaped type, and lined with feathers, etc., when available. The bird is a steady sitter, not easily flushed from her nest. Incubation takes a fortnight, and the young birds leave the nest when about three weeks old. The young birds are of a drab gray hue, showing little scarlet. They grow quickly, however, and soon molt into full colors.

Dufresne's Waxbill (*Coccopygia melanotis* or *Estrilda melanotis*)

Description: Crown, gray; back and wings, smoky olive; a black mask encloses the face, cheeks, chin and throat; rump and upper tail-coverts, scarlet; breast immediately below the black mask is white, which color shades off into gray on the underparts; tail, black; beak, black above, red below. The hen lacks the black mask, her head being all gray. Length: three and one-half inches (88.9 mm). Habitat: South Africa.

This delightful little waxbill has been fairly frequently imported to Europe in the past, but is always rather expensive. It has been known to aviculture for a long time, Hagenbeck, of Hamburg, having first received it in 1869. It is a most attractive aviary bird, being very vivacious and tit-like in its movements. In disposition it is amiable and confiding. Unfortunately it is not hardy and should

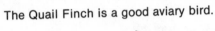

The Quail Finch is a good aviary bird.

be wintered in a warm place. It is also rather short-lived. Though nests are often built, there are few breeding successes recorded.

Quail Finch *(Ortygospiza atricollis)*

Description: Mottled brown above, black on forehead; chin and around the eyes, white; cheeks and throat below the white patch, black; breast and flanks, grayish brown, barred with black and white; abdomen, buff; beak, red; feet, pale brown. The hen has the head and barrings of brown instead of black. Length: four inches (101.6 mm). Habitat: from Senegal to the Sudan.

Quail Finches are strange little short-tailed, terrestrial birds, resembling quail in their habits of running about among the grass. The floor of the cage is best covered with granulated peat moss, or shortly clipped turf. Their feet must not be allowed to become diry, as they are comparatively weak. Their natural food consists of fallen seeds, and they are good aviary birds, breeding fairly freely in grassy aviaries. The ordinary seed mixture for small foreign finches suits Quail Finches very well, and they need seeding grass, ant's eggs, greenfly, etc. The nest is built in clumps of grass, and the eggs usually number five. They are rounded in shape and pure white in color.

Scaly-crowned Finch *(Sporopipes squamifrons)*

Description: Dove gray above, black on the crown with gray margins to the feathers; area between eye and beak, black; white below, with chin and a streak on each side of the throat, black; wing coverts, black, bordered with white; flights, brown, with ashy borders; tail black, with broad white borders; beak and feet, flesh color. The hen is similar. Length: four inches (101.6 mm). Habitat: South Africa and from Angola to Rhodesia.

The Scaly-crowned Finch is a most attractive little weaver, though without bright hues in its plumage. It was first brought to Britain in the last century, but has never been a plentiful species on the market, though obtainable from time to time. It is a free breeder, and was first bred by Mr. W.E. Teschemaker, who states, "This charming little bird has proved as easy to breed as the Zebra Finch, and it is as hardy as it is handsome."

In disposition this weaver is active and noisy and is inclined to be a bit quarrelsome. It makes an untidy, dome-shaped nest in a bush, and will sometimes use a hollow log or covered nest box. The usual number of eggs is five or six, and these are olive or gray, heavily blotched with dark brown. The young birds resemble their parents when they leave the nest, except that the scaly crown is replaced by a patch of brown, and the black between the beak and eyes is absent. Sexing this species is difficult, but the usual guide is the mustachial streak. This is generally larger in the cock than in the hen.

IX Grass-Finches, Parrot Finches and Mannikins

The term "Grass-finches" embraces the graceful, colorful Australian finches, which together with the parrot finches form a most important group of cage and aviary birds. They are not, however, a well-defined class, some of them resembling typical mannikins and others coming very close to the waxbills.

These splendid finches are more eagerly sought after by aviculturists than any group of birds, in spite of the very high prices they now command in Britain and the United States, and the uncertainty of success with some species.

There is no doubt that they are delicate on arrival, though they are now imported by air and often arrive in better condition than formerly. On the other hand, the quicker travel does not give the birds time to become adjusted to changed temperatures. All these birds live in a warm, dry climate, very different from that of Britain and the eastern and northern parts of the United States.

Newly imported birds should therefore be caged up, in fair numbers if possible, as they then keep each other warm at night. The temperature should be high, at least seventy-five degrees Fahrenheit, but you can safely keep them in a cage heated up to ten degrees above that mark. Give the birds cuttlefish and rock salt to nibble, the usual seed mixture of canary and millet, spray millet, and a bath of warm water. These birds are fond of bathing, and it does them no harm if you keep them warm. The heat in which they are kept can be gradually reduced to that of an ordinary living room. Do not put the birds in an outside aviary until late spring, when the cold weather is well past. Aviary bred and acclimatized specimens are fairly hardy—quite hardy in all parts of Australia—but in England and similar climates they are best brought indoors about the end of October until spring.

Nearly all the species will breed in aviaries or even large cages,

A white Rice Finch.

but some are prone to egg-binding, as indeed are all small foreign finches—especially during cold, damp spells of weather. Another trouble with these birds is that they often refuse to conform with our seasons; they will breed too early in spring or not until the following October and onward. They require a nest box about eight inches by six inches by five inches, with an opening of about two and one-half inches at one end. A twist of hay should be placed in this, and more grass or hay supplied to the birds. If it is desired to attempt breeding these birds in cages, Gouldians, Zebras, and possibly Stars, Parsons, and Long-tailed Grassfinches are the most likely subjects among the Australian kinds. The cages should be about three feet long, twenty inches wide and eighteen inches high. Suitable cages could be made out of packing cases, as these birds do not require expensive or elaborate cages for breeding purposes.

Feeding is simple. The stock seed mixture should consist of one-half part canary, one-half part white millet, and one part *Panicum*. Seeding heads of grasses are a necessary item in the bill of fare, but they are not much interested in insects. If you can dig up some small ant's nests with plenty of eggs and put these in a shallow tin tray in the aviary, the birds will enjoy eating them. These birds feed their young on food pre-digested in the crop, and sponge cake, bread-and-milk, and as much seeding green grasses and chickweed as you can supply are all they need—with few exceptions—to rear their young.

Gouldian Finch *(Chloebia gouldiae)*

Description: Top and sides of the head are scarlet, edged with a very fine black band; chin and throat, black; behind the black band on the nape a rather broader band of turquoise blue; breast covered with a large, clean-cut patch of deep, rich purple; rest of underparts, deep golden yellow; back and wings, green; tail, black with two central feathers drawn out into fine needle-like points; beak, white, red at tip; legs, pink. The hen has a lilac-colored breast. During the breeding season her beak becomes dark, grayish slate. Length: five inches (127 mm). Habitat: tropical Australia, from Queensland to northwestern Australia.

The Gouldian Finch has often been called the most beautiful bird in the world, and it is a prime favorite with aviculturists, in

184

The Gouldian Finch is a beautiful bird that favors warm climates.

spite of the fact that it is a tricky bird to manage. Newly imported it is delicate, but once acclimatized it is surprisingly hardy (if kept, day and night at a temperature of about 30ºC) and under suitable conditions it will even winter outside without heat, although this is not advisable at all. If you wish to breed in winter, then artificial heat must be given (30ºC), though Gouldians are not particularly prone to egg-binding.

It is very distressing to lose these expensive, lovely birds, but every breeder has had this trouble. Young birds are particularly likely to fall ill when they reach their first molt and are getting their color. It is best to cage them up in a warm place at this period. Unfortunately, they color very slowly and may take nine months or so to acquire adult plumage.

Gouldians will breed readily in a good-sized box-type cage, about three feet in length, and some pairs are quite prolific. They lay from three to about eight eggs, with five or six as a usual clutch. The eggs hatch out in a fortnight, and the chicks have luminous warts on the side of the beak, which enables their parents to feed them in the dark of the nest.

The young birds in their first plumage are sage green above and grayish below. The immature hens are bigger than the cocks, and of a lighter gray on the breast. The change into adult plumage is slow, and perhaps a year may elapse before a young Gouldian gets his full plumage. The young Gouldians apparently molt at the same time each year—early summer—and if they have been only a couple of months on the wing may only come half way through the molt, remaining in this immature state of plumage until the following year. Birds of both sexes will breed before they attain full plumage.

Once settled down to cage or aviary, the Gouldian breeds freely. Excellent results have been achieved in Australia by breeding on a community system, provided that plenty of extra nest boxes are available.

The Gouldian Finch is tri-chromatic, there being three color varieties—Red-headed, Black-headed, and Yellow-headed. The last-mentioned is exceedingly rare in a state of nature, but has been bred in some numbers of late years. A variety in which the green of the beak is replaced with blue has appeared in Australia, and in that country there are a very few albino Gouldians. No hybrids are known.

Long-tailed Grass-finch (*Poephila acuticauda*)

Description: Top of the head and nape, pale gray; cheeks, silky white; lores, black; chin and throat patch, jet black; back and wings, light fawn; a black band extends across the lower back to the top of the legs; upper tail coverts, rump and abdomen, white; tail, black, with two central feathers drawn out into fine needle-like points; beak, yellow; legs and feet, red. Length: four and one-half (114.3 mm). Habitat: Northern Territory and northwestern Australia.

The Long-tailed Grass-finch is a beautiful little bird, though its hues are not brilliant, and it is seen to the best advantage in an

The Long-tailed Grass-finch is an attractive species; it is native to northern Australia.

aviary, where it is active and interesting. In display it has a curious bobbing motion of the head, usually accompanied by the expansion of the black bib feathers. The sexes are very alike, but the hen usually has a smaller bib than the cock. It is often very delicate when newly imported, and specimens frequently develop diarrhea, shivering, and finally die in a fit. But it is a fairly hardy bird when acclimatized. Aviary-bred birds are the best to purchase. It is best to winter these birds in cages in a bird-room. They are great lovers of the sun, and in the aviary on not too warm but sunny days they usually crouch down in some sunny, sheltered spot.

The Long-tailed Grass-finch breeds quite readily in an aviary, or even a large cage, using a nest box. It lays from four to six eggs. It is fond of live food, and will readily eat gentles, etc.

There is a sub-species of this bird which has a blood-red beak, known as Heck's Grass-finch (*P. a. hecki*). It can be crossed with The Yellow-billed form. Hybrids have been produced between the cock Long-tailed Grass-finch and the Masked, Double-bar and Zebra Finches. In Australia this bird goes by the appropriate name of "Blackheart," in reference to the heart-shaped black bib.

Parson Finch (P. cincta)

Description: Head, silver gray; beak, throat patch, and a streak from the base of the beak to the eyes are black; back, fawn, more brown on the wings; a black bar over the rump; upper tail coverts, white; tail, black; cinnamon on the breast and underparts; black patch on the flanks; white under the tail; feet, reddish. Length: four inches (101.6 mm). Habitat: south Queensland and northern New South Wales.

The Parson or Black-throated Finch is a lovely bird, being somewhat like the Long-tailed Grass-finch, but rather richer in tone, and, of course, it has a shorter tail. The sexes are easier to distinguish than those of the Long-tailed Grass-finch, the hen having a different shade of head color. The cock shows a very light silvery gray, whereas the hen is dull gray hue. The black throat-patch of the hen is rather narrower, and straighter at the sides.

The Parson Finch is known as a bad traveler, and has a very limited range in Australia, which probably accounts for the fact that its appearance on the market is very erratic. It is not too easy to obtain even in Australia, as all native birds are protected in New South Wales and Queensland. The Parson finch has unjustly been given the reputation for being a bit of a busybody, interfering with other birds' nests. But it is natural for these birds to have a nest on hand in which they spend the night. They will soon utilize a nest box stuffed with hay, and sleep in this, eventually using it for breeding purposes. The Parson Finch is not normally pugnacious, indeed, it is often a very gentle bird. Some individuals, however, chase other small birds during breeding. Four to five eggs are usually laid. The young birds are well looked after by their parents, who take them back to the nest each night.

Hybrids have been produced between the Parson Finch and a number of other birds; the commonest hybrids are with Heck's, Long-tails, and Masked Grass-finches. It has also crossed with Bengalese and Zebra Finches.

It can be safely kept in a garden aviary from May until September, after which it is best caged where the temperature does not fall below about fifty degrees Fahrenheit.

Parson Finches are very fond of insect food and should be supplied with gentles and a few meal worms. A form with the upper-tail coverts black is found in north Queensland, referred to as Diggle's Finch. It is uncommon in captivity.

Masked Finch *(P. personata)*

Description: Light chestnut above; beak pale yellow, surrounded by a black mask; crown deep brown; cheeks, neck and underparts rosy brown, becoming white under the tail; a black band across the lower back to the flanks; upper tail coverts white; legs pinkish. Length: five inches (127 mm). Habitat: northern Australia.

This grass-finch is an excellent aviary bird, being a good mixer with other small birds, fairly long lived, and of active and lively disposition. It is a very good breeder generally speaking, some pairs being more prolific than others. Some pairs will desert their nest if disturbed, so no interference should be the rule with sitting birds. Five or six eggs form the usual clutch, and the nest is a flask-shaped ball of dry grass, built in either nest boxes, brushwood, or in growing shrubs in the aviary. The cock bird shares the task of building the nest and incubating the eggs. A curious habit of this bird in the wild state is that of putting small bits of charcoal in its nest. The first breeding record was by Mr. W.L. Hawkins (England) 1900.

The sexes are much alike, but the hen is perhaps slightly smaller, especially about the head. Young birds are very much darker in color than their parents when they leave the nest, and have the beak and feet black. They lack the characteristic mask of the adults, but the change of plumage soon takes place.

In a wild state this attractive finch is common in coastal districts where it inhabits grassy flats near streams. In the breeding season it is met with in flocks of about a dozen or so, but during the dry season much larger numbers visit the water holes in company with other birds.

The White-eared Grass-finch *(P. p. leucotis)* is a sub-species confined to the extreme north of Queensland. Because of its rather remote habitat it has always been extremely rare in collections, but with the gradual opening up of the Cape York district it is more likely to appear on the market. It is much lighter, richer cinnamon brown color than the Masked Finch, having white ear-coverts and

A collection of Zebra Finches.

white below the black of the throat. Its beak is a much paler yellow.

Zebra Finch *(P. guttata)*

Description: Ashy gray above; tail, black barred with white; cheeks, pale chestnut; a white mask surrounded by a narrow black band below the eye; throat and upper chest, silvery gray, finely barred with black, and the whole separated from the underparts by a black band; underparts, white, cinnamon on the flanks, with white spots; beak, orange; feet, salmon. The hen is brown above, gray on the crown, and plain buff below, with a black and white barred tail. Length: four to four and one-half inches (101.6-114.3 mm). Habitat: Australia, mostly inland districts.

Young Zebra Finches; the birds shown are about two weeks old.

This is the best-known of all Australian finches, and is a perky, hardy, pompous little bird with a ridiculous song sounding like the piping of a toy whistle. Several pairs (but never two!) will live amicably together and breed in an aviary, but in this case there should be nesting boxes to spare, otherwise pairs may select the same box and waste most of the breeding season bickering over its possession. The most suitable size of nest box for this small finch is about six inches by six inches by four inches from front to back, with a two-inch wide opening all along the upper front. Hang the nest box near the roof of the cage to prevent the birds making a nest on top of it. Grass and hay are suitable nesting materials, and they will line it with feathers. Staple diet for Zebras should be canary and millet seed. They are fond of green food. Heads of small annual meadow grass should be supplied. For cage breeding a suitable size of cage would be about thirty inches by eighteen inches by twenty inches.

There are quite a number of varieties of Zebra Finches, and new ones are always being recorded. The pied type is gray with white flight feathers and body patches varying from twenty-five to fifty percent. The fawn pied is similar except that there are fawn pat-

A male gray Zebra Finch.

An adult male Zebra Finch (left) and three young.

ches instead of gray. In the marked white the body color is white with chestnut flanks and faint, black-barred chest.

White Zebras were first bred by Mr. A.J. Woods, of Sydney, who reared three young ones in an aviary containing a mixed collection in 1921. They were later established by another Sydney fancier, Mr. H. Lyons, who obtained his initial stock from Mr. Woods. Color variations of the Zebra have turned up before, and even Dr. Russ, the German aviculturist of the nineteenth century, mentions them. Russ, however, attached no importance to these sports, and did not attempt to retain them by line breeding.

Both parents share the duties of incubation, which takes twelve to fourteen days. The young leave the nest in about a fortnight, and are self-supporting in another ten to twelve days. They should be separated from their parents at five weeks, or they will disturb the old birds by crowding into the nest boxes. Young Zebras resemble their mother, but have black beaks. They assume adult plumage within a few weeks.

Star Finch *(P. ruficauda)*
Description: Forehead, cheeks and throat, vermilion, dotted

A pair of Zebra Finches, free breeding and energetic birds; the male is at left.

with white on the cheeks; back and wings, light olive; upper tail coverts, wine red, with white spots; tail, deep rufous; breast and flanks olive, heavily spotted with white; belly, pale lemon yellow. The hen has much less red about the head, and is more gray on the underparts, without the lemon hue. Immature birds resemble the hen. Length: four inches (101.6 mm). Habitat: northern and northwestern Australia.

This lovely finch has become extinct in New South Wales where Gould found it, "Rather thinly dispersed, on the banks of the Namoi River." It is fairly common in suitable localities in tropical Australia, which are reedy places near swamps or streams.

There is a considerable difference in the richness of coloring in birds from different localities. The Queensland form is not nearly so pretty as that from northwestern Australia. This form is very pale both in body color and on the head, showing little red. The western race is rich green above, with a rich vermilion facial blaze, and rich yellow underparts. The white spots are clear and distinct. Aviary-bred specimens in Australia are generally a mixed race. The young birds are dull smoky with black beaks and brown legs when they leave the nest, and the change into adult plumage is rather slow. The coloring of adult birds seems to become more intense with age.

The Star Finch is one of the best aviary birds, being inoffensive to other birds, very lively and will breed well in mixed company or in a colony. It seems to do equally well in large or small aviaries. It will build in a nest box, preferring a cylinder of half-inch mesh wire netting to a wooden box. More often the nest is built in a thick bush, where such accommodation is available, as in a planted aviary with an open flight. The natural nest is built of grasses and is domed with a side entrance. Often the first egg can be seen through the nest which is added to as egg-laying continues. The clutch varies from three to six; live food is absolutely essential. A number of hybrids have been bred with the Star Finch. A handsome cross is that between it and the Crimson Finch; while the Zebra X Star Finch is quite attractive, showing characteristics of both parents.

Diamond Sparrow *(Zonaeginthus guttatus)*

Description: Forehead and crown to the nape, pale, silky gray; back and wings, mouse brown; rump and upper tail coverts, brilliant scarlet; tail, jet black; below white, a broad black band crossing the chest and continued along the sides, where it is boldly marked with large, round, white spots; beak, crimson; feet dark gray. Length: about five inches (127 mm). Habitat: south Queensland to southeastern Australia.

The Diamond Sparrow or Diamond Fire-tail was one of the first birds to attract the attention of the early settlers in Australia, and paintings of it date back to 1790. It is an inhabitant of the drier country, though also found in lesser numbers near the coast. It is much rarer than formerly, and consequently no longer the cheap bird it once was.

In captivity it is hardy when established, lives well and is easy to keep, but it is not a particularly easy bird to breed. Unfortunately,

A Diamond Sparrow is not an easy bird to breed.

it is difficult to tell the differences in the sexes. The most reliable guide is the size of the head. The skull is broader and larger in the cock bird, and the black belt across the chest is perhaps a little broader. Other differences have been mentioned, but they are not reliable.

Diamond Sparrows like to have a nest box lined with hay in which to sleep. They will sometimes roost in this during cold days or inclement weather. If not provided with plenty of boxes from which to choose, the birds are apt to camp in the nests of other birds in the aviary. This can, of course, be disastrous. But the Diamond Sparrow is not at all pugnacious in disposition, merely boldly assertive at times. To get the birds into breeding condition it is advisable to give them plenty of grass seeds, both green and dry. If the grass is gathered when green and abundant and tied in a loosely woven bag, it will dry out and the seed may be shaken loose and stored.

In disposition the Diamond Sparrow is active in an aviary, but old birds are apt to become rather phlegmatic in a small cage, and eat until they become overly fat. It is an ardent and amusing wooer, and the antics of the cock when dancing before the hen are extremely grotesque. It cares little for live food, and young can be successfully reared without it.

Fire-tailed Finch (Z. bellus)

Description: Forehead, lores and around the eyes are black; dark brown above, barred with fine lines; upper tail coverts, crimson; tail and under coverts, black; silvery gray below, finely barred with black; abdomen, black; bill, red; feet, brown. The hen may be distinguished from the cock by the fact that the center of her abdomen is barred like the rest of the under plumage. Length: five inches (127 mm). Habitat: coastal districts of New South Wales, Victoria, Tasmania, and the larger Bass Strait Islands.

This is a not too common finch on the Australian mainland, preferring cool, mountain gullies where it lives in the thick scrub. It is the most difficult of Australian finches to maintain in captivity, the birds dying without any apparent reason. It is very rarely imported, and seldom seen in Australian aviaries. Nevertheless it has bred in captivity, usually building its large grass nest in a thick shrub or pile of brushwood. It has been known to use an ordinary nest box. Except that it is extremely nervous in disposition, the Fire-tail resembles the Diamond Sparrow in general habits.

Painted Finch (Z. picta)

Description: Brown above; rump and tail, scarlet; face, chin, and throat scarlet; breast, flanks and belly, black and spotted with white; an irregular band of scarlet down the middle of the body; beak, upper mandible, black tipped with red; lower mandible, red with blue base; legs grayish. The hen has a black throat, whereas in the cock this is always scarlet. Length: four and one-half inches (114.3 mm). Habitat: central and northwestern Australia.

197

The Painted Finch inhabits the most desolate parts of Australia, but is not uncommon in small parties in grassy places near waterholes and creeks. It was practically unknown to aviculture until about 1935 when small numbers began to reach the English bird markets.

This lovely finch is now being regularly bred in captivity, both in Australia and other countries, and is an ideal aviary bird. It is very tame in disposition and quite harmless to other birds. At liberty these birds build their nests in spinifex or porcupine grass. During the rainy season this grows so rapidly that a nest built in it would be pushed out of shape. To prevent this, the birds' natural habit is to make a platform in the bush with earth, pieces of charcoal or clods from a white ant's nest. They will even collect a small bucketful of such materials. On this they construct the nest proper of dry grass of the usual finch pattern. From four to six eggs are laid, and both birds incubate them. The young birds are apt to squat on the ground after leaving the nest, and the adult birds often do this, sunning themselves on bare ground like fowls. This finch does best in a wood-floored aviary, with the whole of the roof covered. It is essential that no long wet grass be allowed to grow if the birds have access to an open flight. They are subject to chills under such conditions. There do not seem to be any records of hybrids between this and any other finch. Its note is a loud twittering, and the cock has a faint twittering song. Painted Finches are fond of small grass seeds, and take little or no interest in live food. However, some may be taken when they have young to feed.

Bicheno Finch or White-rumped Bicheno Finch (Poephila or Stizoptera bichenovii)

Description: Crown, nape and back, light brown, finely barred with darker; wings, black, with numerous round white dots on the flight feathers; tail, black; rump, white; forehead and sides of the crown, very dark blackish brown; two fine black bands across the neck and breast; sides of head and throat, white; underparts also white, sometimes with a distinct buff tint; beak gray. The hen is slightly duller on the crown and the white between the chest bars is less clean. Length: four inches (101.6 mm). Habitat: northwestern Australia, north Australia, Queensland, and inland parts of New South Wales.

The Bicheno Finch, also called White-Rumped Bicheno, is a friendly but delicate bird.

When newly imported this charming little finch is rather delicate, and it is considered a bad traveler, so that many specimens arrive in a rather rough condition. It does not like cold winds, and is fond of basking in the sunshine. It is a very gentle bird in an aviary, and a suitable companion for small waxbills. In disposition it is very sociable, and a pair will sit side by side preening each other's feathers in a most affectionate manner. The Bicheno is fairly long-lived, but is not too free a breeder in English aviaries, though it breeds fairly readily in Australia in captivity. Young are reared without live food, but soft food and some live food should be given if available. Young Bichenos are dull editions of their mother, devoid of wing spots, but they quickly color and are in full color in about three months.

Hybrids have been produced between the Bichenos and other finches, including Star Finch, Plumhead, Zebra, Parson and Pectorella. There is a sub-species of this bird called the Ringed Finch

(*S. b. annulosa*) in which the rump is entirely black. It is mostly found in northern and central Australia.

Plumhead or Cherry Finch *(Aidemosyne modesta)*

Description: Crown of the head is purple-red, with a bloom like that of a ripe plum; upper parts, brown spotted with white on the wing coverts; upper tail coverts, brown barred with white; tail, black, the outer feathers having a white spot at the tip; chin, dark wine red, almost black; sides of the face, neck, and rest of under-parts are white, barred neatly and regularly with brown; beak, black; feet, light brown. The hen is duller and lacking the throat patch and cherry crown. Length: four inches (101.6 mm). Habitat: Queensland, New South Wales, Victoria.

The Plumhead is a very charming and attractive finch, not too frequently imported nowadays. It likes dry country in its native land, and has not proved at all hardy in an oudoor aviary in England. It is not regarded as a free breeder, but has bred on a number of occasions. It is good tempered in disposition and a suitable companion for any other small finches. It generally builds in a thick bush or bundle of fine twigs, but will use an ordinary finch nest box. Four to six eggs are laid and incubation takes about a fortnight. It has hybridized with Masked, Long-tailed Grass, Zebra, and Bicheno Finches.

Crimson or Blood Finch *(Neochimia* or *Poephila phaeton)*

Description: Crown, dark brown; back and wings, paler brown washed with red; tail is very long with brilliant scarlet above and black below; cheeks and the whole of the underparts are deep crimson, spotted with white on the flank; center of the belly and under the tail, black; beak, red; legs, fleshy yellow. The hen is paler than her mate, and has pale gray chest and underparts. Length: five inches (127 mm). Habitat: tropical Australia.

This beautiful bird is commonly called the Blood Finch in Australia, and dealers in the United States know it as the Australian Fire-finch. Unfortunately it has the reputation of savagely attacking and killing other small birds, especially those showing red in their plumage. It is evident, however, that this is not true and there are indeed many cases of these birds being safe-

200

The Plumhead or Cherry Finch is not a hardy bird and is not frequently imported.

ly kept with other small finches. But it would be as well, on turning Crimson Finches among other birds, to watch them very carefully, and for some time, as they are sometimes vicious in the wild.

This lovely finch is not a beginner's bird. It is a lover of heat and sunshine, and in climates like that of Britain it needs some heat in winter, though it is more intolerant of cold, damp weather, rather than just low temperatures.

A pair kept in a large cage or aviary on their own, or with birds too large to be bothered by the cock's possible attacks, the Crimson Finch is a lovely and interesting bird. No finch is a better subject for a small aviary in a conservatory or one end of a glassed-in veranda. It can stand almost any amount of heat.

The nest is a sparrow-like structure of grasses, lined with feathers, which should always be supplied to breeding birds. The birds will readily use a good-sized, finch nest box, budgie nest box, or any suitable structure. In northern Australia these birds build under the eaves of houses and other buildings.

The display is impressive, and when performed in full sunlight the plumage seems to be on fire. The tail is spread out fanwise and the body held very erect. The cock makes a curious low sound and moves his head slowly from side to side in a most odd and dignified manner.

The Crimson Finch was first bred in Germany in the closing years of the last century. Some successful cage breedings have been recorded. Live food should be given when breeding, and in Australia fanciers breed this bird without much difficulty in districts where termites can be obtained. Gentles and a few meal worms might be suitable substitutes. The young birds are quite unlike their parents, being dark brown with black beaks.

Pin-tailed Parrot Finch *(Erythrura prasina)*

Description: Top of the head, back and wings, bright green; rump and tail, red, with the central tail feathers elongated into fine needle-like points; chin, cheeks, face, and throat, dark blue; underparts, rich golden brown, becoming decidedly reddish on the breast; beak, black; feet, flesh color. The hen lacks the red and blue on the throat, which is a mixture of brown and green.

The Pin-tailed Parrot Finch, otherwise known as the Pin-tailed Nonpareil, is a delicate bird. It has not yet been bred in captivity.

Length: five and one-half inches (139.7 mm). Habitat: from Burma through Malaysia to Sumatra and Java.

The Parrot Finches *(Erythrura)* form a small group of extremely lovely little birds in which the plumage is very rich parrot green, red and blue.

The Pin-tailed Parrot Finch, sometimes called the Pin-tailed Nonpareil, is fairly often imported from Singapore, but in the past birds have arrived in rather poor condition on many occasions, and have proved delicate and difficult to establish. They are fed on paddy rice (rice in the husk) in their native land, and it is often difficult to get them on to canary seed. This, together with rye grass, millet, and a few oats, is a satisfactory staple food.

This bird does not seem to have been bred in captivity, and apparently its natural breeding arrangements are not recorded. It can be kept in an outdoor aviary in summer, but in winter should be kept in a temperature of about fifty degrees Fahrenheit as a minimum.

Red-headed Parrot Finch *(E. psittacea)*

Description: Head, throat, and upper part of breast, vermilion red; rump and tail also of the same striking hue; rest of plumage, glossy parrot-green; beak, blackish; feet, gray. The hen has less red on top of the head. Length: five inches (127 mm). Habitat: New Caledonia.

This magnificent finch is a great favorite with aviculturists, but it is rare today, since it is protected in its only home, the island of New Caledonia, lying some 800 miles off the Queensland coast. But the birds are good breeders, and stocks have been maintained in Europe and Australia by keen aviculturists.

The Red-headed Parrot Finch is an excellent aviary bird. Its brilliant plumage is most attractive, and its flight is very swift, like a painted arrow shooting past. It has not proved quite hardy in Britain, however, and in winter is best where the temperature does not fall below forty-five degrees Fahrenheit. It is perfectly harmless to other small birds.

When in breeding condition, the cock commences to utter a curious little song—a loud prolonged *"chee,"* which is followed by a creaky trill resembling someone winding a clock. For breeding purposes it will adopt almost any kind of nesting receptacle, preferring a wooden box with a hole in the side, or a hollow log. The cock builds the nest and sits during the day, while the hen incubates at night. Incubation takes fourteen days, and the young leave the nest when about three weeks old. They are drab green, with only a little red on the face. The birds are fond of bathing, and this helps to keep their plumage in good condition. Diet should be canary and millet, and they are fond of sweet apple.

Blue-faced Parrot Finch *(E. trichroa)*

Description: General body color is a rich dark green above, slightly lighter below, tinged with golden olive on the flanks; top of the head, cheeks, and face to the ear-coverts, dark cobalt blue; rump and tail, dull carmine; bill, black; feet, pale brown. The hen is similar to the cock, but the forehead and cheeks are a much duller blue in color. Immature birds are uniform green, without the blue about the head. Length: four and one-half inches (114.3 mm). Habitat: first discovered in the Caroline Islands. Now known to inhabit many islands in the southwest Pacific, and the mainland of New Guinea. A few have been taken in northern coastal areas of Australia.

Though not so brilliant as the last species, this is a very desirable aviary bird, being quite a free breeder and easily maintained. It will nest either in a bush or more frequently in an ordinary finch nest box. The usual clutch numbers five, and the incubation period fourteen days. The birds are normally very good parents, and the young birds are ready to leave the nest when about three weeks old. They are fed for about ten more days after leaving the nest. The young birds should be removed from their parents when they show their adult colors. This is when they are about three to five months old, depending on the season. The Blue-faced Parrot Finch will raise brood after brood if allowed to do so, but breeding should be discouraged after about four nests.

The cock bird is easily recognized, apart from the rather bright blue of the head color, by his note. This is a trill whistle, whereas the hen's call is simply "zit-zit." Feeding is simple, the birds are fond of canary seed, white and spray millet, and green food, such as half-ripe oats, wheat or barley, and rye grass. They like fresh ant's eggs and a few meal worms.

Royal Parrot Finch *(E. regia)*

Description: General body color is bright, deep blue; top and sides of the head, rump and tail, brilliant scarlet; wings, green; beak, black. The hen has more green in her plumage and the red areas are duller. Length: about four inches (101.6 mm). Habitat: New Hebrides.

This very brilliantly colored bird differs in shape from the other parrot finches, being short-tailed, plump, and stocky in build. It is nervous in disposition and takes a long time to become steady in a cage, being perhaps better suited to life in an aviary. It is, however, susceptible to cold, and liable to die for no apparent reason. It must have more fruit than other finches, and the diet should consist of canary and millet seed, spray millet, soft food, and plenty of apple.

The Royal Parrot Finch was first imported and exhibited at the London Zoo in the spring of 1934. It was first bred by Dr. C.H. Maclin, of Ampthill, Bedfordshire, in 1935.

A (pied) Rice Bird.

An immature gray Rice Bird.

MANNIKINS AND MUNIAS

The Mannikins and Munias are a group of small Asiatic and African finches with large beaks and coarse feet, but close and sleek plumage of plain but pleasing colors. They are excellent aviary birds, but not so interesting when kept in cages, though they will thrive equally well in either. They are sociable in disposition, hardy, and long-lived.

Some kinds are ready breeders, but others are not at all willing to nest. They require covered nest boxes with a hole in the side, or they will build a domed nest in a bush. They are usually difficult to sex, the colors being much the same in both cocks and hens. The cocks, however, have some sort of song, though there is often more gesticulation than audible notes in their performance.

Their feeding is very simple. The seed mixture should be canary, white and Indian millet, spray millet and green food. When rearing young, they should have soft-bill mixture, bread-and-milk and soaked seed, or sprouted seed.

Java Sparrow or Rice Bird *(Padda oryzivora)*

Description: General body color, delicate pale gray; head, black except for a large, pure white patch on the cheeks; tail, black; beak, pink; feet, flesh color. The hen is slightly smaller, the crown narrower, the beak more regularly tapering and not so deep at the base. Length: five and one-half inches (139.7 mm). Habitat: Java and Bali, the other Indonesian Islands, China, and introduced into many warm countries.

About the size of an ordinary sparrow, but much more sleek and smartly clad, with an outsize, bright pink beak, the Java Sparrow is a great favorite. It is one of the birds that can be safely associated with budgerigars, but it is not really a safe companion for birds smaller than weavers.

A Calico Rice Bird.

Gray Java Rice Bird with black cheek patch.

The wild Java Sparrow is not a free breeder in captivity, but the white variety does so quite freely. The typical, or Gray Javas, are usually bred by crossing the white with the ordinary kind. The results of such a mating will reproduce their kind quite readily, but prolificacy varies with individual pairs. White Javas are more popular than Grays and command a ready sale.

An ordinary budgerigar nest box is suitable for Java Sparrows, and this they line with hay and feathers, laying from four to six white eggs. These hatch in a fortnight. The young are fed on regurgitated seeds by their parents, and though it is usual to give some soft-bill food, this is not really necessary. But seeding grass, green food and cuttlefish bone should always be offered.

Black-headed Mannikin (*Lonchura atricapilla*)

Description: Body color is a deep, rich chestnut brown; head and breast, belly, and under the tail, black. The hen is slightly duller and more brownish on the underparts; she is rather small and has a longer and narrower beak. Immature birds are dull brown, tinged with rufous on the rump; chin, throat, and abdomen are buff white. Length: about four and one-half inches (114.3 mm). Habitat: India, Burma, and Malaysia.

This is one of the most popular of foreign finches, and is a good bird for the beginner, being hardy and pretty in a quiet way. Its efforts at singing are very amusing; after much gesticulation the cock emits a faint squeak, exactly like the mew of a kitten heard from a distance. It often builds a nest and lays eggs, but is a rather restless sitter and rarely brings up any young.

The Three-colored Mannikin *(L. malacca)* is very similar but prettier, the breast being pure white, contrasting nicely with the black and chestnut of the head and back. It is confined to central and southern India and is not so common on the market as the last mentioned species. It rarely breeds, and the sexes are similar.

The White-headed Mannikin *(L. maja)* is chestnut with a white head and a neck tinged with buff. The hen is more smoky in coloring about the head. It comes from Sumatra and Java and is very long-lived—one having survived eighteen years in captivity—but it rarely breeds. The most likely reason is that northern climates are not hot and humid enough to induce nesting. The three birds described above are called Nuns, while the present species is known as the Cigar-bird in its native land, its white head on the brown body being compared to the ash on a half-smoked cigar.

Spice-bird or Nutmeg Finch *(L. punctulata)*

Description: General color is chocolate brown, darker on the head; below, is light brown, becoming white on the abdomen; feathers of the breast and flanks edged with dark brown, producing a scaly appearance. The sexes are colored alike, but the beak of the cock is thicker and heavier than that of the hen, and his head is also larger and broader. Young birds are light brown without any markings. Length: four and one-half inches (114.5 mm). Habitat: India and Ceylon.

This is one of the most commonly imported of Indian birds, and is to be found in almost every collection of finches. In its native land it is a common bird of gardens and cultivation, and frequently builds its large, sparrow-type nest in creepers and trellis work in gardens. Indian bird dealers sometimes dye these birds green, not to deceive customers, but to make the birds more attractive. The Spice Finch is not at all a ready breeder in captivity, but hybrids between it and other finches have been produced. It has crossed with the Bib Finch, Bronze Mannikin, Silverbill, Black-headed

210

White-headed Mannikin.

Bengalese (Society) Finches breed better in a cage than in an aviary.

Mannikin and Bengalese. The Spice Finch is an attractive bird in its quiet way and may safely be associated with any small finches, provided they are not overcrowded—and, indeed, most aviaries contain at least twice as many birds as they can conveniently hold. There are several species which differ slightly in the mottling of the breast. One which is fairly well known in aviaries is the Malay Spice Finch *(L. topela)*, which is not so attractive as the Indian bird, being duller in color.

Bengalese or Society Finch

The Bengalese is a domesticated bird and exists in three varieties—pure white, white irregularly marked with buff, and white marked with chocolate brown. Besides these there is a crested type, obtainable in all these colors. This bird was originally produced centuries ago by the Chinese and is believed to have resulted from a cross between the Striated Finch and the Sharp-tailed Finch.

A quietly fascinating little bird, quite unpretentious in either mannerisms or coloring, the Bengalese has certain pleasing traits which make it an extremely popular cage bird. It is one of the few foreign birds which will breed better in a cage than in an aviary, and it is a valuable foster parent for hatching and rearing the young of grass-finches. It is hardy and can be kept in either cage or aviary. If kept caged indoors at ordinary living room temperature it may be allowed to breed at any season, but in an unheated aviary it is better to keep the sexes separated during the winter to avoid the danger of egg-binding.

Unfortunately, the sexes are alike, and cocks can only be determined when they are seen displaying to the hens. This they do with an amusing bowing motion, uttering their harsh, squeaky little song. Bengalese are sociable and of an amiable temperament both with their kind and with other species.

The Sharp-tailed Finch (*L. acuticauda*), already mentioned as one of the ancestors of the Bengalese, is a native of India, Burma, and Sumatra. It is reddish brown, darker on the crown and upper back, face and throat; underparts are sandy, streaked with gray; wings, dark brown; tail, black; beak and feet are dark gray. It is hardy and long-lived, but not so easy to breed as the Bengalese, except when crossed with it.

The Striated Finch (*L. striata*) is marked in a more contrasting way. The belly and rump are purer white, while the head and breast are dark bronze-brown, almost black. It comes from southern India and Ceylon.

African Silverbill (*L. cantans*)

Description: Grayish brown above, darker on the head; all the feathers with pale borders; wings and tail are blackish brown, the tail being long and pointed; underparts, sandy buff, white in the middle of the abdomen and under the tail; rump, black; beak, blue-gray. The hen is said to have a lighter colored bill, and narrower skull but otherwise resembles the cock. Length: four and one-half inches (114.3 mm). Habitat, southern Arabia, northwest Africa from Senegal across to East Africa.

Though soberly colored, this is a particularly charming little bird and a great favorite with all fanciers. It is a lively little bird, and the cock has a habit of warbling faintly at frequent intervals.

The song of the cock is the surest indication of sex, as the hens are colored in a similar way. Young silverbills are more uniform in color, and begin to assume their adult plumage when about three months old.

The silverbill is very easy to breed in an aviary or large cage using the usual finch type nest box, with the entrance at one side. The domed nest is made of grass and feathers, etc. It has produced hybrids with several closely related munias. Silverbills are perfectly harmless to other birds. If caged, a pair should always be kept together. It is fairly hardy when acclimatized.

The Indian Silverbill (*L. malabarica*), which occurs from the Himalayas to Bengal and southward to Cape Comorin and Ceylon, is darker on the upper parts, this being earthy brown. It has a white rump; tail, blackish and rather long and pointed; rest of plumage is pale buffy white, faintly barred on the flanks; bill, brown, faintly tinged with lavender below; feet, pinkish purple. The cock is slightly purer white on the breast than the hen and a bit richer in color tone, otherwise similar.

This species of silverbill is easily kept on millet, *Panicum*, and green food, and breeds fairly readily in cage or aviary. The usual clutch of eggs is four, and incubation lasts thirteen days, the young birds leaving the nest at about twenty-one days. Soft food in the form of plain cake and soaked bread should be provided when they are rearing young. Live food is also much appreciated. There are fawn varieties of both Indian and African Silverbills. The Indian Silverbill has crossed with the African species, the Zebra, and Cherry finches, and possibly other allied birds.

Cut-throat or Ribbon Finch *(Amadina fasciata)*

Description: General body color is light fawn, each feather marked with a small black bar; belly, chocolate; tail, gray; throat, whitish, crossed by a necklace of vivid crimson; beak and feet, light flesh color. The hen lacks the red throat band and the chocolate abdomen. Length: four and one-half inches (114.3 mm). Habitat: Africa, Senegal across to the Sudan, Kenya and Tanzania.

This popular finch is one of the best known foreign cage and aviary birds, and though not a gaudy species is a good breeder in

The Cut-throat or Ribbon Finch gets its name from the red bar found across the throat.

either cage or aviary. It should be provided with a covered nest box and some hay and feathers when it starts to build. The hens are very susceptible to egg-binding in cold weather, and this is the one snag in building up a stock of these birds.

Two or three broods are often reared in the summer, and newly imported birds can be put outside about the end of May, and they can then remain through the winter without artificial heat, the Cut-throat being a hardy bird. It is not much of a songster, but the cock has a low bubbling warble. The normal note is a sparrow-like chirp.

The Red-headed Finch resembles the Cut-throat Finch but differs in the distribution of its pattern of markings; it also is a bigger bird.

Food should be a staple mixture of canary and millet seeds, with soft-bill mixture and gentles when rearing young. Live food should be supplied regularly after the young birds are hatched. The chicks grow quickly and leave the nest about three weeks after hatching and are able to fly at this stage. The cocks have the scarlet band in the nestling stage, and the birds will breed when about three months old. In warm climates they will breed throughout the year. About three to six is the normal clutch, but as many as eight young have been reared at a time in Australian aviaries.

Cut-throats have been rightly accused of interfering with other birds' nests and bullying smaller birds, although on the whole they are suitable birds for a mixed collection of small finches, but it is important that the aviary is not overcrowded. They can be kept and bred on the colony system.

The Red-headed Finch (*A. erythrocephala*), sometimes called the Aberdeen Finch, is larger than the Cut-throat and somewhat resembles it, but the cock has the whole of the head crimson, and no collar. It comes from Angola down through western parts of southern Africa, and is often offered on the market. It breeds quite freely in captivity and has hybridized with the Cut-throat. The hybrids are fertile, as is the case with practically all hybrids.

The Magpie Mannikin is the largest of the African munias.

Magpie Mannikin (*Lonchura fringilloides*)

Description: Back and wings dark brown; head, rump, and tail, black; glossed with steel green; breast and underparts, pure white; sides of the body mottled with black and buff; tail, black. The hen is slightly smaller than the cock, with a narrower beak. Length: about four and one-half inches (114.3 mm). Habitat: central and northwest Africa.

This rather large mannikin is a suitable companion for Java Sparrows and Weavers, and has bred in an aviary. It is hardy, but has the reputation of being a bully, which is an overstatement.

Bronze Mannikin (*Lonchura cucullata*)

Description: Brown above, black on the head and throat; white below, mottled with gray on the flanks; tail, black; rump and tail coverts, buff with dark brown bars; a metallic green patch on the shoulder; beak leaden gray, upper mandible darker. The hen is a little less glossy and browner above, and has a narrower head with a more regularly tapering beak. Length: about three and one-half inches (88.9 mm). Habitat: from the coast of West Africa across to the Sudan.

This is one of the most active and vivacious of the mannikins, which are a somewhat sluggish group of birds, and the most interesting of them to keep in a cage. Though hardy, it has rarely bred in Britain, but is said to have often done so abroad. In 1907, Mrs. Wesley T. Page bred a hybrid between this species and the Magpie Mannikin.

A number of other members of the genus *Lonchura* have been imported.

The Bib Finch (*L. nana*) is about the size of a Gray Waxbill and is a suitable companion for very small finches. It is earthy brown, with a black chin; underparts, gray, mixed with brown on the belly. Sexes alike. Coming from Madagascar, it is not a common bird, but is a good breeder for a mannikin.

The Black-and-white Mannikin (*L. bicolor*) is mostly black, glossed with bronzy green, with the lower breast and rest of the underparts pure white. The beak is bluish. It is a native of west Africa and is not often seen in captivity. Reputed to be a fairly good breeder on the continent and not too quarrelsome in an aviary.

The Rufous-backed Mannikin (*L. nigriceps*) is also rare and comes from East Africa. It is similar to the last, but has chestnut back and wings, the sides black lined with white, and the flights and rump black with white spots.

Yellow-rumped Finch (*L.* or *Donacola flavipyrmna*)

Description: Back and wings are chestnut brown; crown and nape, gray, whitish on cheeks; rump and upper tail coverts, golden buff; throat and breast, buff, washed with fawn on the flanks; black under the tail; beak and feet, bluish gray. Length: about four inches (101.6 mm). Habitat: north and northwestern Australia.

The genus *Donacola* contains three birds generally spoken of as Australian Mannikins. They are sometimes (although not correctly) distinguished from the typical Grass-finches (*Poephila*) by their shorter tails, thick-set and rather stumpy bodies and stout beaks. Though not gaudily colored they are very popular with the more discerning aviculturists, the present species being the least common but the most ready breeder of the group. The Yellow-rumped Finch was unknown to aviculture until 1904, when a few specimens were trapped. A pair of these found their way to the Melbourne Zoo, and a single bird was sent to England. Since that time it has been imported in small numbers, and is not too difficult to obtain nowadays.

The Yellow-rumped Finch is an inland species, only appearing on the coast during times of exceptionally severe drought, otherwise living in desert country. It was first bred in 1906. The nestlings are darker in color than their parents, having a dark brown head, throat, back, and tail, and dull gray chest. They attain adult plumage within three or four months. A hybrid between this and the Chestnut-breasted Finch has been bred in Australia.

The sexes are alike, but the hen is slightly smaller than the cock, and paler in color. The head of the hen is rather flat on the skull, whereas that of the cock is more rounded. The head color is lighter buff in the cock.

The Yellow-rump is a very quiet type of bird, quite inoffensive to other birds and other pairs of its own species. It takes rather a long time to settle down in an aviary, and it may be a year or so before pairs show any signs of wanting to nest. The nest is large and untidy, made entirely of grasses without any special lining.

Four eggs are the usual clutch. Incubation takes a fortnight, and the young birds become independent about three weeks after leaving the nest. Both parents share the task of looking after the young. Food should consist of mixed seed, live food—gentles, ant's eggs and meal worms—seeding grasses and stems of silver beet. The call note of this bird is like the tinkling of a tiny bell.

Chestnut-breasted Finch (*L. castaneothorax*)

Description: Crown and nape are gray with dark streaks; back and wings, dark cinnamon; rump and upper tail coverts, orange yellow; tail, straw color; cheeks and throat, black; breast, rich chestnut; underparts are white marked with black along flanks and under the tail. The hen is slightly paler. Length: about four inches (101.6 mm). Habitat: northern Australia, extending into New South Wales.

Called the Barley Sparrow in northern New South Wales, this handsome finch is mostly found in grassy places near rivers. It destroys cereal crops and is considered a pest. It is an excellent aviary bird, being amicable, long-lived, and interesting in its ways. The display of the cock consists of the bird drawing himself up to his full height and then hopping rapidly up and down on his perch while facing the hen.

It is not a very ready breeder in captivity, but has hybridized with several mannikins, the Striated Finch, Indian Silverbell, Masked Grassfinch and Zebra Finch. Some of the hybrids are fertile. One of the offspring of a cross between this bird and a Black-headed Mannikin paired with a Spice Finch and reared young.

Pictorella Finch (*L. pectoralis*)

Description: Light gray above, tail darker; a narrow buff line over the eye to the sides of the neck; sides of the head and throat are black; broad white band across the chest, with a few black bars on the feathers; rest of underparts, pinkish gray with white bars on the flanks; beak, ash gray; feet, flesh color. The hen is very like the cock but has the feathers on the sides of the face, ear-coverts and throat of a brownish black hue, instead of the glossy tint in the cock. The hen has a narrower skull. The breast feathers are slightly different. In the cock the breast is barred horizontally black and white, while the hen shows more white than black. Length: four inches (101.6 mm). Habitat: throughout northwestern Austrlia, Northern Territory, and north Queensland.

This is probably the prettiest and best known of the genus, and is a popular cage and aviary bird. It was first imported to England in 1896, and was bred for the first time by Mrs. Howard Williams who successfully reared a brood in 1905. The birds nested in a rush basket, and an account was published in the *Avicultural Magazine* for December, 1905.

The Pictorella has been bred many times since, but it is not regarded as at all easy to breed. Many pairs never show any inclination to nest. The nest is a bulky structure of grasses, and built near the ground as a rule, sometimes in a tussock of grass. Three to four eggs are laid, and incubation lasts a fortnight. Both birds take part in the brooding. The chicks remain in the nest for three weeks after hatching. When they emerge they are plain brown and cannot be sexed. Though not normally nervous, the Pictorella is a touchy bird when on the nest, and any interference with the nest or handling of the eggs would probably cause the birds to desert them.

When feeding young they will take live food, and are partial to gentles, especially in the pupa stage. The usual seed mixtures and seeding grass should be given. Several pairs will live amicably in the same aviary.

The Pictorella Finch is susceptible to cold and should not be exposed to extreme cold and damp in winter; but it is not delicate, and does not need coddling.

Index

Page numbers set in **bold** type refer to illustrations.